MW00512056

ROB KAPLE

WIND
WORDS

waking up to a new conversation
about God, yourself and the world.

Rob Kaple's website: http://www.robkaple.com
First Edition
Designed by Kirby Kaple

Library of Congress Cataloguing-in-Publication Data available upon request.
ISBN-13: 978-0-9984899-0-2

CONTENTS

Are your ears awake? Listen. Listen to the Wind Words,
the Spirit blowing through the churches.

THE MESSAGE

A QUESTION

If you were to meet yourself on the street, would you recognize your own face?

Someone asked me this question recently. It sounds ridiculous, but think about it for a second. We're used to looking at ourselves in a mirror. Most of us assume that when we gaze at our reflection, we are seeing ourselves as everyone else does, but in reality, we're seeing a reversed image.

If you look in the mirror and wink with your left eye, the person in the mirror winks with his or her right eye. If you take into account that nobody's face is perfectly symmetrical (I may have just ruined your life with that statement), and that you only ever see your reflection at a fixed angle in a mirror, you'll realize that everyone else's experience of your face, your body, your mannerisms, and the weird shape of your head might be totally foreign and unrecognizable to you.

Let's try a little experiment. Go look in the mirror. Seriously. Get up, go into the bathroom, and check yourself out. I'll be here when you get back.

No surprises there, right? Except maybe for the piece of spinach in your teeth.

Let's try another experiment. Pull out your phone and turn on the video feature. Now flip the camera so it's facing you. (If it's already facing you I'm silently judging you for taking too many #selfies.) If you're in an airport or a library (do people still go to libraries?) or a mall food court (you should probably pause and grab an Orange Julius and an Auntie Anne's pretzel), you're not excluded from this exercise. Apologize to the people around you in advance and buckle up. It's gonna get worse before it gets better.

I want you to hit the record button and start singing the Oscar Meyer Wiener theme song ("Oh I wish I were an Oscar Meyer Wiener . . ."). As you sing, rotate the camera around your head from the middle to the farthest left that your arm will reach, and then rotate it all the way back across to the far right. Nice and slow. Arms fully extended. Now get an angle from up top. Then from down below, looking up at your chin.

If you don't know the Oscar Meyer song, substitute one of the following 1990s pop hits: "Livin La Vida Loca" by Ricky Martin, "Boomtastic" by Shaggy, or the rap portion of "Waterfalls" by TLC ("I seen a rainbow yesterday . . ."). Actually, I just looked up the lyrics to "Boomtastic." I should probably remove that as an option.

Now watch the video. What do you notice?

You look weird while you're singing, don't you? Especially from the side and from above or below.

You look different than you do in the mirror. Now imagine what you look like to all those people sitting around you waiting for an airplane or trying to read a book or eat their Sbarro calzone in peace.

Most of us picture ourselves based on what we see in the mirror every morning, but other angles exist. The world around us is experiencing something much more dynamic than what we see while brushing our teeth or in that quick glance at a passing storefront window to make sure our hair isn't all jacked up.

Let's be honest. If you bumped into yourself at your favorite coffee shop, you would probably still recognize yourself, even if it took a few seconds. Your face, your voice, your gestures— they would all be eerily familiar and at the same time, foreign. The person in the mirror, the person you're used to seeing, is the real you. It's just not the *whole* you.

Our perspective is limited, but that doesn't mean a greater reality does not exist.

Most of us have been handed down specific ways of viewing God, the Bible, ourselves, other people and the world in which we live. We've received these perspectives from our parents, our friends, our favorite television shows, and our religious (or not so religious) upbringing. We all have a different point of view, and no one's outlook is perfect. We've spent most of our life looking at each of these areas from a fixed position, like our reflection in a mirror.

Throughout human history, God has been helping people gain a new perspective. A new way of seeing. We glimpse this in the lives of individuals in the Old Testament, such as Abraham, Jacob, Moses, and David. We see it in the way Jesus interacted with his disciples and the way the Holy Spirit moved in the early church in the New Testament.

The Apostle Paul's sentiments never rang more clearly: "For now, we see only a reflection, as in a mirror; then we shall see face to face. Now I know in part; then I shall know fully, even as I am fully known."

Let me tell you one quick story from the New Testament as

an example.

ROOFTOPS AND REPTILES

One day, as he was sitting on a rooftop waiting for supper, the Apostle Peter started to pray. He fell into a deep trance and had a vision of a sheet being lowered down from heaven by its four corners. In the sheet was every sort of wild animal, even the ones that were considered "unclean" and, therefore, forbidden to be eaten under Hebrew law. Then Peter heard the voice of Jesus command him to "Kill and eat."

"No way!" Peter retorted. (I'm paraphrasing here.) "I've never eaten anything that you have said is unclean!"

"Don't call anything unclean that I have called clean!" Jesus replied.

This apparent argument between Peter and the Creator of the universe went on, and Jesus said the same thing three different times. (Three is kind of an important number in the Bible, by the way.)

While Peter was wondering about the vision, three men (there's that number again) from the house of a man named Cornelius knocked on the door looking for a man named Peter, whom an angel had told Cornelius about. Just then, the Holy Spirit spoke to Peter and told him to go with those men.

Cornelius was a God-fearing Gentile, which means he was not Jewish, which means he was an outsider, even in the eyes of the growing Jesus community at that time. Peter went with the men to Cornelius's house and shared the good news about Jesus. As he spoke, every member of Cornelius's household was filled with the Holy Spirit, so Peter decided it would probably be okay to baptize them with water (sounds logical).

Later on, Peter had to defend his actions to the rest of the church leaders, because it was illegal for a Jewish man to enter a Gentile home. Up to that time, the growing New Covenant church was still abiding by certain Hebrew laws and had not considered that God might want to do the same thing among the outsiders (Gentiles) as he was doing among them, the elite, insider community.

That moment—on that rooftop, looking at that sheet— changed the world.

If not for that sheet, the message of Jesus of Nazareth might never have left that small Jewish community. It may never have spread across the Roman Empire. I probably would not have been told, as a sixteen-year-old, that I could have a personal relationship with Jesus. You probably wouldn't be reading this book or even be living in the same country!

If Jesus had not confronted Peter with a different angle on something so familiar, Jesus' command to go to the "ends of the earth" may never have become a reality.

LISTEN

In the book of Revelation, Jesus gave John, the disciple whom he loved, a special message to share with seven local churches throughout Asia Minor (essentially, where Turkey is today). He concluded each of the seven letters with the same question and statement. I like how Eugene Peterson phrases it in *The Message*:

"Are your ears awake? Listen. Listen to the Wind Words, the Spirit blowing through the churches." (The Message)

Across the Old and New Testaments, and throughout history, these Wind Words, the voice of the Spirit, have been blowing through the communities of God's people. In each new generation and context, God says something fresh, peeling back the surface to reveal previously unknown layers of his plans, his desires, his nature, and the reality that Jesus calls the "kingdom of God."

Peter hears the words "Don't call anything unclean" on a rooftop in Joppa in the first century and brings the Good News of Jesus to the Gentile world.

The Council of Nicaea gathers in the third century, forming the modern canon of scripture, allowing future generations to access God's heart in the Bible.

St. Francis of Assisi abandons a life of luxury to identify with the least of these in thirteenth-century Europe, inadvertently starting a movement within the Catholic Church and becoming the namesake of today's Pope.

Martin Luther nails his ninety-five theses to the door of All Saints Church in Wittenberg, Germany, in 1517, exposing the corruption of the religious powers of his day and catalyzing the Protestant Reformation.

The nineteenth-century American abolitionists give their lives to end slavery in the United States, leading a young nation one massive step closer to "liberty and justice for all."

Nelson Mandela spends twenty-seven years in prison in the late twentieth century for advocating racial justice in South Africa, eventually becoming that nation's president at seventy-five years of age, bringing an end to the oppression of apartheid.

The history books are filled with people who partnered with the heartbeat of God to impact religion and culture as they listened to the Spirit and labored toward this reality. People whose hearts were open. People whose ears were awake.

People who acted on the Wind Words.

I believe these Wind Words are always speaking. The Spirit is always moving. Jesus is always writing a letter to his churches. Expanding our perspective. Teaching us how to see.

My primary purpose in writing this book is not to tell you what these Wind Words are but to begin a conversation in the hope that you might find yourself in the company of those who listen . . .

and then act.

This is a book of questions before it is a book of answers. Questions you're terrified to ask out loud. Questions you may have pondered silently in your bed at night or dared to ask a family member or a leader in your local church, only to be warned that you were stepping onto a slippery slope. Questions you can't shake no matter how hard you try.

And the first question might just be the most important.

Are your ears awake?

CHAPTER ONE

·· · · · · · · · ·

WORD

Last summer, my wife, Kirby, and I spent a week in Colorado in the middle of the Rocky Mountains with some friends. That cool mountain air was a much-needed change from the muggy humidity of Atlanta in July. In fact, I didn't sweat all week until the moment we touched down on the tarmac, back home in Georgia.

While we were there, I spent an afternoon fly fishing on the winding river at the entrance of Rocky Mountain National Park with a few of my friends—Drew, Matt, and Pat. This probably sounds really manly and outdoorsmany (that's a made-up word a true outdoorsman would never use), but you should have seen us out there. At one point, a few local fishermen walked past with judgment and disgust in their eyes, and for good reason. Matt had altitude sickness and could barely walk, Pat was wearing bright blue swim trunks and a ladies' raincoat (I have no idea why), and I couldn't catch a fish if it jumped into my pocket. At one point in the afternoon, I realized I didn't even have a fly on my line anymore. I was just out there waving a pole around with some loose string on the end thinking I was "getting my form down." The only one of us who looked like he knew what he was doing was Drew, and that's because he had spent the entire summer in the mountains leading a discipleship program for college students (and he's a little more outdoorsmany than the rest of us).

None of us caught anything all day (big surprise), except for Pat, who, to our amazement, was able to swipe a fish right out of the water with a net! We were all really impressed— until he let it go and it just sort of floated upside down for a while. I think it was dead before he caught it!

LEARNING TO KNOW

In Philippians 3, the Apostle Paul gives a stern warning against anyone who puts confidence in the *flesh*, i.e., religious practice. The word *flesh* here is tricky. Sometimes in the New Testament, this word is used as a substitute for "sinful nature." That's not the case in this passage. Paul uses the Greek word *sarx*, which basically speaks of anything natural or physical about a person, like our physical abilities or strength, family heritage, house, job, or personal competencies. Basically, anything about yourself from which you might be tempted to derive your identity or self-worth.

That day as we were fly fishing in Colorado, I can honestly say I put no confidence in my own *sarx*.

Paul goes on to say that he used to be one of those people who thought a lot of his *sarx*, and then gives a list of reasons why.

"If someone else thinks they have reasons to put confidence in the flesh, I have more: Circumcised on the eighth day, of the people of Israel, of the tribe of Benjamin, a Hebrew of Hebrews; In regard to the law, a Pharisee; as for zeal, persecuting the church; as for righteousness based on the law, faultless."

Paul is saying he used to derive all of his pride and confidence from his role in the community in which he grew up. He could trace his ancestry so far back into the Jewish narrative that he knew which of the twelve sons of Jacob from which his family line came. He was an original Hebrew. A true insider. If someone wanted to come in from the outside and be a part of *his* elite community, he or she would *never* belong to the degree Paul did.

"But whatever was to my gain, I now consider loss for the sake of Christ. What is more, I consider everything a loss because of the surpassing worth of *knowing* Christ Jesus my

Lord . . . I want to *know* Christ."

Paul is basically saying, "I used to put confidence in my abilities, but now I just want to know Jesus." The Greek word for *know* used here is *ginosko*. This word is translated as, "to come to know, to perceive, to feel, to be known." It's an intimate, relational word. It was actually used as a Jewish idiom for sexual intercourse.

Yeah, I have your attention now.

Intimate.

It's the word the gospel writers used to describe Mary, the mother of Jesus, when they said she didn't *know* a man until after Jesus was born.

Get it?

My favorite definition for this word is "to learn to know." Isn't that great? Paul is saying, "I'm on a journey. I'm not there yet. I'm just getting started in this whole *knowing* Jesus thing."

I feel that way about Kirby. We've been together for over ten years, and I'm just scratching the surface. I'm still "learning to know" her.

Paul is saying he used to derive his confidence, his self-worth, and his "righteousness" from his personal religious practices and the role they afforded him in the community. Now he just wants to *know* Christ. He used to *know* all the answers. Now he just wants to *know* a person.

He is speaking about the difference between knowing *about* someone and actually *knowing* them.

Religion versus relationship.

I know *religion* is an interesting word, and I realize there are a lot of good things about religious practice, so at the risk of oversimplifying a complex idea, I'll use the word *religion* to describe empty routine, self-righteousness, or hypocrisy. Going through the motions.

It's what Brennan Manning referred to as, "the temptation of the age . . . looking good without being good."

WWJD?

Recently, Kirby bought me an issue of *GQ* magazine. She does that occasionally. I think she wants to inspire me to expand my fashion sense. She also saves pictures of clothing that she thinks I'll like to a Pinterest board that I'll never see, because, strangely enough, I'm not on Pinterest. (No, I'm not a Pinterest hater, but if I want to be bombarded with shirtless images of Ryan Gosling, I'll just watch *The Notebook* like any other self-respecting guy.)

As I was leafing through the magazine, I noticed a picture of Kanye West stepping out of a car wearing a little black bracelet with "WWJD?" embroidered on it in white.

I'm pretty sure we're all familiar with the "What Would Jesus Do?" trend of the mid-1990s, so it's no surprise when we see one of those bracelets every now and then. It's kind of like when you stop at a red light behind a dusty, old Ford Taurus with a hundred Beanie Babies piled up against the back windshield. Some people just kept rocking them well into the twenty-first century!

What was strange about the image is that most people probably don't associate Kanye with Christianity. (I guess he did have that one Jesus-y song early on, but the music video for "Gold Digger" permanently erased that imagery from our mind.) We certainly would not expect him to ask himself the question those four little letters represent.

That's the funny thing about being an "insider." Eventually, we give ourselves the task of determining who is on the "outside." Religion always likes to know where everyone else stands. In fact, if you want to find the most religious person in the room, look for the person with the most answers. (I'm that person more often than I care to admit!)

That little black bracelet with the white letters on it got me thinking.

There's an early church legend about the Apostle Peter from the time he spent in Rome. According to the legend, Peter had been undergoing great persecution during his ministry there and decided to flee the city to escape his likely execution at the hands of the Roman government.

As he was leaving, he passed by the risen Christ. Startled, he stopped and asked his Savior, "*Quo Vadis*?" That's Latin for "Where are you going?"

Jesus responded by saying he was going *into* the city to be crucified again! Shocked, and probably a little ashamed of himself, Peter turned and followed the Lord back to continue his ministry in Rome, where he was eventually crucified.

This has become known as the legend of *Quo Vadis*.

Where are you going, Jesus?

Is this story true? I don't know, but it's a powerful illustration of what it looks like to follow Jesus.

Through the years, I have heard pastors and teachers apply the legend in many different ways. Some have used it to inspire people to follow Jesus out into the mission field.

Others have used it to challenge congregants to be willing to lay down their life for the cause of the gospel, to become martyrs, much like Peter did.

These are useful applications of the legend, and I am in full support of sending more missionaries out into the field, but when I hear this story, I hear a slightly different message.

I don't think the most important part of the story is *where* Peter followed Jesus to or *what* he ended up doing for Jesus. I think the most important part is the *question* Peter asked.

"*Quo vadis*?" Where are you going, Jesus?

I'm not so sure Jesus is looking for martyrs. Martyrdom is a big deal. The scriptures are clear that great honor in the age to come awaits those who have made the ultimate sacrifice for the sake of the gospel of Jesus, so I'm not making light of that at all. But when I hear that story, I don't think, "Jesus wants us all to be martyrs for our faith."

I don't think Jesus is looking for martyrs, missionaries, or pastors. (I'm a pastor, by the way.) I think Jesus is looking for people who are willing to ask the right questions.

"*Quo vadis*?"

Where are you going, Jesus?

Religion is about having all the right answers, but relationship is about asking the right questions.

Where are you going, Jesus?

What are you saying?

What are you doing?

WWJD? bracelets were a huge trend in the 1990s, and, apparently, Kanye is bringing them back, but I'm thinking about making a bracelet of my own.

WIJD? (What Is Jesus Doing?)

What if we learned to ask that question? We don't have to decide for ourselves what Jesus would do *if* he was living in our neighborhood, working our job, or sitting at our dinner table. He's here, and he's speaking, moving, and walking up those marble stairs back into the city that we might be evacuating.

"Quo vadis?"

Where are you going, Jesus?

WORD(S)

One passage of scripture has haunted me over the past few years. It comes from John 5:39–40.

"You diligently study the scriptures because you think that by them you possess eternal life. These are the scriptures that testify about me, yet you refuse to come to me to have life."

Jesus was rebuking the Pharisees, those who dedicated their lives to memorizing and living by every detail of the Torah and the Prophets, because they were so focused on the words on the page that they missed the Word made flesh standing right in front of them.

What a challenging couple of verses!

I have studied the Bible daily since I was in high school. I love the Bible! I believe the words on the page, because I believe they are God-breathed. I believe they are alive. They have come alive in me!

I also recognize that far too many churches and preachers speak of the Trinity as if it consists of Father, Son, and Holy Bible!

Don't get me wrong; I love the Bible, but we need to understand what the Bible is. As Westerners in the twenty-first-century, we have a tendency to take the Bible for granted and make big assumptions about it. If we're not careful, we'll begin to think that it fell out of the sky bound in leather and gold-leafed with a built-in ribbon for a bookmark. (If you ask me, you don't see the built-in bookmark ribbon enough these days. I say we start putting them in other books, too. Maybe this book!)

The fact is, the Bible is not a book.

The Bible is a library of books.

Sixty-six books, to be exact. This library of sixty-six books was written by forty different authors on three different continents over a period of more than two thousand years. (Google it!)

God didn't physically write the Bible. He didn't sit down at his desk one day with a feather quill and inkwell and start composing on a scroll. People did that as they experienced God and life and love and disappointment and tragedy and joy. The scriptures were written by the hands of men as they encountered God.

Not a book. A library.

An amazing library though! In fact, by human standards, it's nearly impossible that a library of books with such a diversity of authorship, dates of composition, and cultural context could have such unity from start to finish. A common thread, an ongoing narrative, runs throughout it. It's an incredible library that tells an incredible story about an incredible God who revealed himself in an incredible man named Jesus.

The Bible is all about Jesus. It's always been about Jesus. It will always be about Jesus. So, when Jesus (whom the Bible is about) interacted with people who were obsessed with certain parts of the Bible (remember, the last bit hadn't been written yet), he was justifiably frustrated with them for their massive exercise in missing the point.

That's what religion is, by the way. An exercise in missing the point. Making an end out of the means.

Now that we are all on the same page (see what I did there?) about what the Bible is, let's talk about what the Bible does.

Sitting on my desk as I type right now are four different Bibles. I didn't put them there to make a point; that's just where they are today. Some are big, some are small, some are new, and some are tattered and falling apart. Each of them has served me well throughout different seasons of life. To my left is the Bible I purchased when I was seventeen years old, a senior in high school, on fire for God. In the margins are all sorts of thoughts and revelations I wrote down as I pored over those words through the years. The pages are wrinkled from carrying it through the rain. Verses have been highlighted and underlined. Ink has bled and smudged. I think I spilled some honey mustard in there at one point. Throughout those pages are passion and history and intimacy with God.

Amazingly enough, that particular Bible is still intact. The one I bought in college is in pieces though! Same model (thin line). Same translation (NIV). Same color (navy blue)! Zondervan must have decided to save some money and switch to a lower quality glue after 2003. Or maybe that first Bible was supernaturally preserved by the sustaining power of God, much like the clothing and shoes of the Israelites as they wandered through the desert. (That's a Bible joke. It won't be the last one. Go ahead and settle in for the long haul.)

Either way, I'm thankful my first Bible is still in usable condition. Sometimes I still preach from it for old times' sake or take it to a coffee shop or on a hike at Stone Mountain. Reading from its yellowed pages is like catching up with an old friend.

But I'm not the same person I was when I purchased that Bible.

As I've read and wrestled with those words and experienced life and love and pain and sadness, I have changed. I look back at the stuff I wrote in the margins (a sort of journal of a zealous young adult), and I realize I don't even believe some of those things anymore! As I've read those words, I have come to know the *Word* better.

John talks about the Word like this:

"In the beginning was the Word, and the Word was with God, and the Word was God. He was with God in the beginning. The Word became *flesh*, and made his dwelling among us."

There's that word again.

Sarx.

I could probably write another entire chapter about why that's important, but we'll keep moving forward.

The Greek word for *Word* here is *logos*. It describes a message or an idea. It's where we get the English word *logic*. It's as if John is saying, "There's this message, this statement, this idea about God, that he has been communicating about himself for all of eternity. It's the truest thing about him. It is who he is."

And when that *logos* is wrapped in our *sarx*, it looks like Jesus of Nazareth.

When God speaks, we see Jesus.

Often, we read the Bible and pull out helpful principles for living a holier or healthier or more prosperous life. We love principles. Principles are easy. Principles are clean and stable and fixed. Principles can be helpful, but the Bible was never supposed to be about principles.

The Bible is about a person.

A relationship.

Relationships are different from principles. Relationships are messy and dynamic and fluid and wonderful.

BIG MO

The Apostle John says in John 1 that the law was given through Moses, but grace and truth came through Jesus.

Moses is a really important guy in the history of God's interaction with his people. The book of Numbers says Moses was the humblest man on Earth. Of course, it's traditionally believed that Moses wrote the book of Numbers, so I don't know if it counts if you say it about yourself. (Nice try, Moses.)

In all seriousness, Moses knew God better than anyone else

at that time in history. Exodus 33 says God would speak to Moses face to face, as one speaks to a friend. In that same chapter, Moses, while up on the mountain with God, made a bold request of his almighty friend. I'll paraphrase.

Moses: "Hey God, we've been hanging out together for a while now. We talk face to face, but I want more. I want to see your glory!" (I guess this is sort of the Old Testament version of "Let's take this relationship to the next level.")

God: "Sorry, Mo (oh yes I did), but no one can see my face and live. (I thought Moses was already meeting with him face to face? The Bible is confusing sometimes, people. Let's embrace the mystery!) But I know a place on the side of the mountain where there's a cave. You can sit in it. I'll cover you with my hand and then allow all of my goodness (whatever that means) to pass by you. Oh yeah, and I'll also yell my name, 'The LORD' (*Yahweh* in Hebrew) out loud, and I'll let you peep at my backside as I walk by."

That little encounter with God caused Moses' face to shine so much that the Israelites were afraid to go near him.

Just one glance at God's backside.

Some think the phrase "face to face" used earlier in that chapter was just a figure of speech used to communicate the type of interaction Moses had with the LORD. Their relationship was intimate, familiar. But Moses was well aware that more of God was yet to be revealed, which is why he made his request.

Moses' revelation of God came with the glory of a glowing face and a covenant of stone tablets.

The Law was given through Moses.

Grace and truth came through Jesus.

If Moses was seeing God's butt, then Jesus is what God's face looks like. If a glance at God's rear end while he was walking away gave us the law, then grace and truth are what come from staring intently into the eyes of love.

Principles and relationship are as different as stone and skin.

I've prayed that prayer of Moses on many occasions. "Show me your glory!" I've read the accounts in the Old Testament of fire falling on the altar and the pillar of smoke and the parting of the Red Sea and thought, *Wouldn't it be great to experience God like that?*

The short answer is . . . No.

I mean, sure, it was great for them at that time, but Moses' revelation of God pales in comparison to ours. Paul says in 2

Corinthians 3 that the glory of the New Covenant surpasses that of the old and that Moses' radiant face faded, while ours just grows brighter as we stare intently into the face of love.

In fact, Paul says that the more we look at Jesus, the face of God, the more we are transformed into his likeness, shaped into the true, grace-giving image of our Savior with ever-increasing glory.

INTERPRETATION

I love the Bible because it tells me what God is like. It tells me that God is like Jesus. It tells me that Jesus is the image of the invisible God, that he is the radiance of God's glory and the exact representation of his being. It tells me that the law was given through Moses, but grace and truth came through Jesus. It tells me that, at one time, God spoke through angels and prophets, but now he has spoken *by* his Son.

Notice it doesn't say "through," but "by."

Wanna know what God has to say? Look at Jesus. Listen to his teachings. Look at how he lived.

His words, his works, and his *ways*.

Jesus doesn't just reveal the nature of God by the things he says but by the things he does.

I used to think there was only one way to read the Bible, that whatever the person on stage said a passage meant was what it meant. I didn't realize that the preacher could be totally biased, misinformed, or straight up wrong. Now that I'm often the guy with the microphone, I feel the weight of the reality that I could be completely off my rocker, and lots of people could be hearing me say stuff that simply isn't true. I've considered giving the old LeVar Burton challenge at the end of all my sermons: "Don't take my word for it."

I didn't realize then that to *read* the Bible is to *interpret* the Bible. (Did your mind just get blown? Try to sleep tonight. I dare you!)

I didn't realize that whenever we read the scriptures, we make decisions about what they mean, decisions about what God said and is saying.

Even translating the scriptures from one language to another is an act of interpretation. Have you ever been overseas on a mission trip and needed someone to translate for you? It's terrible. I preached at a few churches in Central America several years ago, and it was pretty rough. Everything took twice as long to say, and nobody laughed at my jokes. I realized at one point that the translator was saying different stuff than I was saying! Why? Because she was not a *translator*; she was an *interpreter*. She had to make decisions in the moment about how to interpret what I was saying to a group, whose culture and context I didn't understand, in order to make it make sense to them.

In my mid-twenties, I got my eyes checked, and when the optometrist told me I needed glasses, I was pumped, because I thought glasses looked cool. My prescription was light, but it was enough to warrant some sweet new Warby Parker frames. I wore them for two years, and then one day, on a family vacation, I took them off to wear sunglasses on the beach, and I never put them on again. I guess I didn't need them that badly after all.

This is the way we all approach the Bible (and life, for that matter).

We don't even realize we are wearing glasses. We have a lens, a filter, handed down to us by our culture, our family, our experiences, our personality, and the religious ideas of the people who lived before us. We read the Bible and think that what we think it means is what it actually means, because we can't see our own lenses, our filters, our glasses.

A few years ago, a group of Australian young adults came to stay with us to learn about some of the ways we do ministry at our church. They were a rowdy, fun-loving crowd. They taught me all sorts of Australian slang, and I did my best to pull off a solid "down under" accent. They all laughed, because I ended up sounding like mixture between Crocodile Dundee and Austin Powers.

The funniest part of the week was when they started doing impressions of Americans. Hearing someone with an Australian accent do an impression of me was a strange experience, because in that moment, I realized I have an accent.

Have you ever thought about that? You may think the way you speak is normal and that everyone else sounds funny, but to someone else, you sound funny.

Everyone has an accent.

All of us.

Even you.

No one's tone or dialect or pronunciation is "normal." There is no "normal."

I heard someone say recently that Jesus may live in your heart, but Grandpa lives in your bones.

This is why people can love God and still be a jerk to their spouse or flip out on their kids at the grocery store or give

someone the bird in traffic. This is why we can have members
of the same church freaking out in a Facebook debate about
gun control or immigration or taxes. Jesus and Grandpa
don't always get along, and everyone's grandpa is different.

Simply realizing that we are wearing glasses, that we have
an accent, that we are interpreting the Bible (and all of life)
through our own lens and trying our best to communicate
in our own dialect is a huge step forward. It allows us to be
honest about what we are reading *into* what we are reading.
We may never be able to fully remove the glasses (and maybe
we shouldn't), but we can at least recognize how they color
the way we see.

How many times have we read the Bible, this grand library,
this epic narrative, which was always meant to reveal *the God
who is love*, and painted a picture of him that looked more
like us than Jesus?

I've heard it said that the scriptures act as a sort of
Rorschach Test (you know, the ink blots that psychiatrists
use on TV), which actually says more about us than about
what we are looking at.

If I read the Bible and conclude that God is angry and violent
and petty, that might say more about me than it says about
God.

If you're reading the Bible, and it doesn't look like Jesus, you might be reading it wrong.

If it doesn't look like Jesus, you might be interpreting it wrong.

If your God is not love, you might be missing the point.

So, what do we do with the parts of the Bible that don't make a lot of sense to us? What if we started interpreting the rest of scripture through Jesus rather than the other way around? What if we let the revelation of Jesus have the final say?

There is no plain reading of scripture. There is no flat view of the Bible. We have to give more weight to certain passages over others (and we all do this already, whether we realize it or not), because certain passages stand in stark contrast to others. If we view the Bible with any lens other than Jesus, we might end up with a Christianity that doesn't look anything like Jesus. We might end up with a Christianity that supports all of our pre-existing biases and provides us with ancient views on violence and gender and race and sexuality. That would be weird.

All of this, of course, begs the question, "Which Jesus?" Jesus healing the sick? Jesus teaching in the temple? Jesus chilling with his friends? Jesus flipping the tables? I would argue that the clearest picture of God that we have is Jesus on the cross.

Laying down his life for us.

God is self-sacrificing love.

If you want to know what God is like, look at Jesus on the cross. Let that be your filter. Your lens. The key that unlocks every door you come to throughout the rest of the Bible.

HOLY

One more thought before I conclude this chapter.

In Revelation 4, the Apostle John has a vision of the throne room in heaven. Around the throne are the elders, clothed in white, laying their crowns before the Lord. In the center of the room are four living creatures, or animals, flying around the throne. One looks like a lion, the second looks like an ox, the third looks like a man, and the fourth looks like an eagle (totally normal scenario). Each of the creatures has six wings (similar to the seraphs in Isaiah 6), and they are covered in eyes, even under their wings. (Kind of gross, right? What do you call that space under a wing anyway, a wingpit? Do they have eyelids and eyelashes on all of their eyes? What do you do on a windy day when you're covered in eyes or if someone sneezes on you? I bet it would be really easy to get pink eye. Or dry eye. Okay, I'll stop.)

These creatures are covered in eyes and are flying around

the throne, and day and night, they never stop saying, "Holy, holy, holy is the Lord God Almighty, who was and is and is to come."

The word *holy* actually means, "set apart," "unique," or "different." These creatures are covered with eyes. All they do is look at God. All day. All night. They have enough eyes so that if they have to blink with one eye, they have plenty of other eyes with which to keep a steady gaze. They don't miss a thing. And all day long, they keep shouting, "Different! He's different than we thought! Look at him from this angle. I've never noticed that before. Different, different, different!"

When I proposed to Kirby, I bought her a diamond ring, .66 carats (Impressive, I know!). God is like a giant, precious diamond with countless (perhaps increasing) facets to his personhood, and we, like those weird flying creatures, will have all of eternity to gaze at new, previously unknown angles of his glory, forever declaring "Holy! Different! Wonderful!"

As Richard Rohr says so beautifully, "God is much different than we thought and much better than we feared."

I used to have a lot of answers. I used to know a lot about God. Or so I thought. But, like Paul, I just want to press on to take hold of Jesus. I haven't obtained it yet. Now I have way more questions than answers, and I'm okay with that.

Religion is about having the right answers.

Relationship is about asking the right questions.

I'm just *learning to know* Him.

CHAPTER TWO

· · · · · · · · · ·

FATHER

We've talked about the fact that Jesus shows us what God is like. God is like Jesus. God is love. If you want to know about God, look at Jesus. In fact, any image we have of God that doesn't look like Jesus (especially Jesus laying his life down for both friends and enemies) is, at the very least, incomplete, and at worst, idolatrous.

Jesus reveals God's nature to us by the way he lives and the things he does, but he also tells us about God with his words.

TREEHOUSE

When I was a kid, maybe eight or nine, my dad sat me down and asked me if I would like to have a treehouse. I said *no*. Just kidding. Of course I said *yes*! What eight-year-old boy wouldn't want his very own treehouse?

My dad told me we were going to build the treehouse together. He drew up all the plans and figured out what materials we would need, and then we went to Home Depot and picked out the wood and the nails, the cement for the foundation, and the shingles for the roof (yeah, it had shingles; pretty sweet), and we brought it all home.

Side note: I realize now that my treehouse wasn't actually in a tree, so maybe another word besides "treehouse" would be more appropriate. But this is my story, so I'll call it what I want.

We spent the next few days cutting and nailing and pouring (the cement, of course) and painting, and by the end of the week, I had the coolest treehouse in the neighborhood. It even had a sign that my grandpa made for me, which we hung inside the new fortress. It read "Robby Kaple's Secret Sword of the Ninja Club."

Yes, I went by *Robby* until I turned ten. Then I made the very adult decision to shorten my name to the much more mature and efficient *Rob*.

And yes, I said "Ninja."

It was the early 1990s, and everyone loved ninjas. Every other movie that came out was about ninjas. It wasn't uncommon in those days to see a child walking down the road in my neighborhood dressed from head to toe in ninja gear. My parents even started referring to our house as "the dojo."

That last part isn't true, but that would have been awesome.

And now, the ninjas had a place to meet.

The treehouse.

Let's be honest: I didn't build that treehouse.

My dad said we were going to build it together, but I was eight. He drew up the plans. He picked out the materials. He cut the boards and drilled the holes and poured the cement. If I did anything, it was because he wanted me to learn how to swing a hammer, not because of my knack for working with my hands.

Can you imagine if he had asked me if I wanted a treehouse and then said, "Here ya go, son. All the tools and materials are in the backyard. Knock yourself out! Oh, and be careful with the table saw."

Someone would have called Child Protective Services!

My dad wanted to do something nice for me, and he decided to let me be a part of the process.

NAMES

When Jesus showed up on the scene, he began to introduce a new way of thinking about God.

There are a lot of names for God throughout the Hebrew scriptures. Early on, in Genesis, God is referred to as *Elohim*, which speaks of a ruler or judge. Basically, someone who is in charge.

At other times, the word *Creator* is used to describe Him. Throughout the Old Testament, God is referred to as *Yahweh* or *Jehovah*. Most English translations use the word *LORD* in all caps. Centuries later, the Jewish community considered this name to be so holy that they refused to pronounce it.

When Moses met God at the burning bush, Moses asked for a name. "Who should I say sent me?"

"I Am who I Am," God said. He was revealing to Moses that he is dynamic, on the move. He is not just a static idea or a distant judge. He is the God who *is*. It's almost as if he was saying, "I *am* with you. I *have been* with your people, even through years of suffering and slavery. I *am* the one who will lead you out."

God is the ultimate *being*, and all *beingness* (I'm just gonna keep using made-up words if that's cool with you) flows from him.

So, by the time Jesus walked the earth, these ideas about God were deeply established in the Jewish community. But just as God had been progressively revealing new characteristics of his nature throughout history, he wasn't done yet.

One day, the disciples asked Jesus to show them how to pray.

"Pray like this," he said. "Our father . . ."

Wow! Can you imagine the look of shock on their faces?

Judge.

Ruler.

Creator.

Lord.

The God who *is*.

We can handle these names for God. We can handle these ideas.

But *father*?

This was new territory. Eventually, this language became common among Jesus' disciples. They began to inquire more about this *father* of whom Jesus spoke so freely.

"Show us the father," they asked.

"If anyone has seen me, they have seen the father," Jesus explained.

Not only is God a father, as Jesus reveals, he is a good father. Better than any human father. Better than the best father who gives the best gifts. "If you, then, though you are evil, know how to give good gifts to your children, how much more will your Father in heaven give good gifts to those who ask him!"

I realize that, for some people, the word *father* comes with a lot of baggage. You may not have had such great experiences with your father. I feel fortunate to be able to tell stories like the one I mentioned earlier about my dad. Maybe your father was not so good. Maybe he was abusive. Maybe he was withdrawn and cold. Maybe he was simply absent. This could make it terribly difficult to embrace the idea of God as a loving father. A distant judge might actually be easier to stomach, but it is through this revelation that God intends to heal us.

When Jesus was in the Garden of Gethsemane, facing his

impending crucifixion, he prayed, "Father, everything is possible for you. Take this cup from me. Yet not what I will, but what you will."

This time, he used the Greek word *abba* to address his father. This word has made a lot of people very uncomfortable for a long time! It's a term of endearment. It's what a little girl calls her dad. In English, it is best translated as *daddy*.

Daddy?

A BETTER NAME

A few years ago, I was at a worship concert and found myself sitting in my chair with my eyes closed while everyone else was standing and singing (that happens pretty often actually), and I felt God begin to speak softly to my heart.

"You need a better name for me."

Huh?

"You always call me *Father*."

What do you have in mind?

"What do you call your earthly father?"

That's when it sank in. I've never called my earthly father, *Father*. That would be oddly formal. I can just imagine myself walking into his study (he doesn't have a study) while he is sitting behind a giant mahogany desk (he doesn't have one of those either) smoking a pipe (well . . .), and saying, "Pardon me, Father, but may I present a query?"

I didn't grow up in Downton Abbey.

I call him *Dad*. It's comfortable. When I hear the word *Dad*, a lifetime of memories floods my mind. I hear his voice over the phone asking how work is going. I smell steaks on the grill after a long day on the lake.

When I was a child, my dad travelled for business and would often return home from a flight after my brother, Sean, and I had gone to bed. I remember lying in bed and hearing the garage door open (it shook the entire house) and the sound of Dad's footsteps on the kitchen floor. There's something about the sound of a dad's footsteps. They're powerful. No one else in the family has footsteps like those. There's a force behind them.

I would leap out of bed, run downstairs, and jump up to hug my dad. I remember feeling the cold air that had stuck to his overcoat. That's what Dads do. They brave the cold outside while everyone else stays home, warm and safe.

As I sat in that worship service, I realized that *Father* was such a formal way to address God, and he was inviting me into something more intimate. He was inviting me to be his son. His child.

Brennan Manning talks about the beauty of being the beloved of the *Abba*. "Living in awareness of our belovedness is the axis around which the Christian life revolves. Being the beloved is our identity, the core of our existence." In reference to Jesus' relationship with his father, Manning explains that Jesus invites us into the same "intimate and liberating relationship" that he enjoys.

Intimate.

Liberating.

This is what it means to follow Jesus. This is what it means to be human. This is God's desire for every person who has ever lived, that we may experience the "intimate and liberating relationship" of being our *Abba's* child.

Is that what your relationship with your Heavenly Father is like? If not, it might be time to embrace a better story, to start using a better word. A better name.

Abba. Dad.

PRODIGAL

In Luke 15, Jesus tells a story about the kingdom of God. This has become one of his most famous parables, and for good reason.

"There was a man who had two sons . . ."

This is how Jesus begins the parable, and it's an important statement. The chapter begins with an observation from Luke: "The tax collectors and sinners were all gathering around to hear Jesus. But the Pharisees and the teachers of the law muttered, 'This man welcomes sinners and eats with them.'"

Jesus was surrounded by a crowd of people from two different groups: the religious elite and the "sinners." (I love that there are often quotes around that word in the gospels!) He starts the parable by telling them about a father who had two sons. Both sons were deeply loved. Both of them belonged to their father.

The younger, more ambitious, and rebellious son asked his father for his share of the estate early (Normally that was supposed to happen after his father had died. In essence, by making this request, this son was wishing his father dead!). His father honored his request, and then the son took the money and hit the road. Straight to Vegas.

Drugs, sex, fancy cars, penthouse suites . . . He lived it up
and spent it all, and then the housing market crashed, the
economy tanked, and the only job he could find was at an old
farm feeding pigs. He was so hungry that he wanted to eat
the pig food!

Then he had a lightbulb moment. "I will set out and go back
to my father and say to him, 'Father, I have sinned against
heaven and against you. I am no longer worthy to be called
your son. Make me like one of your hired servants.'"

So, he left the pigs behind and went to see his father

While he was still at a distance, his father saw him and ran to
meet him. The son started his well-rehearsed speech, but his
father interrupted him and placed a robe over his shoulders,
sandals on his feet, and a ring on his finger. Then they killed
a fattened calf (evidently, that was a pretty big deal back
then) and threw a party. They got the best DJ in town, rented
an inflatable bouncy castle, and threw down like there was
no tomorrow.

The older son—who had stayed home, honored his father
through the years, and served in the family business—was
coming in from the fields after a long day's work. He heard
the subs thumping from the pool house and was confused.
When he heard that his younger brother had come home,
he refused to go in and see him. His father came out to meet

him and begged him to come inside to join the party, but the older son was ticked.

"All these years I've been slaving for you and never disobeyed your orders. Yet you never gave me even a young goat so I could celebrate with my friends. But when this son of yours who has squandered your property with prostitutes comes home, you kill the fattened calf for him!'"

"'My son,' the father said, 'you are always with me, and everything I have is yours. But we had to celebrate and be glad, because this brother of yours was dead and is alive again; he was lost and is found.'"

Beautiful. This short parable reveals more about the heart of God than endless pages of discourse and debate ever could. We know it as the parable of the prodigal son, but Tim Keller has famously referred to it as the "parable of the prodigal God."

The word *prodigal* means "wasteful." The son is regarded as wasteful because of the way he squandered his father's wealth. Keller argues that this parable reveals the way the extravagant (or prodigal) grace of God is poured out on even the most "lost" soul.

Both sons were rebelling, manipulating their father for what they wanted, either by breaking the rules or by observing them. Both were lost in their own way and alienated from relationship with their prodigal father.

"There was a man who had two sons."

Both were the beloved of their *abba*.

Both were the objects of their father's undying affection and extravagant grace.

When I first heard this parable in high school, I identified with the younger son—desperate, destitute, aware of my need for God's grace and acceptance. As the years have gone by and I've grown accustomed to the household, this parable speaks to me in new ways. After years of serving God, when I look in the mirror, I am starting to recognize the older brother.

The words of the older son are of utmost importance for those of us who have been serving God for any length of time.

"All these years, I've been slaving for you."

SERVANT AND FRIEND

There is a powerful Greek word, *doulos*, which is translated as "servant" or "bond-slave" in the New Testament. The idea came from the Torah, in which God commanded that all slaves must be set free after six years of labor—with one exception. If the slave loved his master and wanted to continue to serve him, he could become a *bondservant*. When this happened, they performed a ritual. The master would pierce the servant's ear with a boring device all the way through into a doorpost (not making this up), and the freed slave became his servant for life.

The Greek word *doulos* is used throughout the New Testament by the apostles, who referred to themselves as bondservants of Jesus. Even James, Jesus' biological brother, called himself a *doulos* of Christ.

This word is inspiring and challenging as we consider what it means to surrender to God for the sake of his kingdom. In college, several of my close friends decided to get the word *doulos* tattooed on their wrist as a reminder of this lifelong service and devotion for which they had volunteered.

This word has a dark side as well. The older brother tells his father, "I've been *slaving* for you all these years." The word for "slaving" used here is *doulouo*, the verb form of *doulos*. This son's identity and relationship with his father had become defined entirely by his role as a bondservant rather than as a son.

It's so easy to slip into this way of thinking. We are excited to let God use us, and it's rewarding to see how he can do such amazing things through our feeble hands. But Jesus' declaration to his disciples in John 15 has to remain at the forefront of our minds.

"I no longer call you *servants*. I call you *friends*."

Can you guess what word he used for *servant*? Yep, *doulos*.

In their late twenties, those same buddies of mine decided to get a tattoo on their other wrist.

Philos.

Friend.

THE FAMILY BUSINESS

The more I contemplate the message of this famous parable, I realize it can be easy to assume there are only two categories of sonship (or daughtership) in Christ: the prodigal who is coming home or the bitter older sibling. The end goal for the younger brother was not for him to become like the older brother. The goal for both sons is for them to become like their father!

That is the invitation to both the faithful and the failure. Can you imagine how the story would have gone if the older brother had grown to think and love and give the way his father did? He probably would have been watching and waiting for the return of his beloved, long-lost brother as well. He may have even set out on a journey into a foreign land to find his brother and bring him home to his heartbroken father.

If we are to grow into the likeness of our Heavenly Father, we must be eager to search for and welcome our missing brothers and sisters and be excited to celebrate their return. The true sons and daughters of God know how to throw a party! Instead, many of us are judgmental, resentful, and distrusting. We don't know how to celebrate our siblings, because we don't know how to celebrate at all! And we don't know that we are being celebrated as well.

"I am always with you, and everything I have is yours."

Many of us have such an impoverished outlook on our place in the abundant kingdom of the heavens that we live as slaves of our master rather than as children of our father. It's no wonder the older brother wasn't happy to hear the music. The man he viewed as a shrewd master was acting like a loving father toward someone who didn't deserve it.

JUSTICE

Kirby and I don't have any kids yet, but I do have a dad. I

also have a brother, Sean. Anyone with siblings (or young kids of their own) is familiar with the phrase "That's not fair." Within every young child dwells a desire for fairness. Justice. Equality. Not for the sake of other people but for themselves.

Heaven help us if one child gets a little more Lucky Charms in their bowl than the other. Or if one child gets more presents at Christmas. World War III.

I'm four years older than Sean. That means I got to do all the fun stuff before he did. My parents let me pierce my ears when I was fifteen. He was eleven at the time, so no way. I got to move down to the basement in high school, while he had to stay upstairs in his childhood bedroom. I got to go out with my friends on Friday nights, and he had to stay home.

Fairness and justice and all that stuff are really important to children. Not so much to parents. They just want to keep peace in the household and teach their kids to be halfway decent human beings.

Good parents don't punish their kids for the sake of justice. They discipline their kids to help them learn and grow. To teach them what is and is not appropriate behavior as a member of the family and of society.

Why would we assume anything different about God? In his

kingdom, it would seem that restoration trumps retribution.

TRIBES

When we talk about ancient Israel, we're talking about a tribe. A tribal people who lived among other tribes. Israel was also made up of different tribes. Twelve, to be exact.

Each of the twelve tribes was actually attributed to a different brother in the line of Jacob (also known as Israel, the father or patriarch of the Israelites). These various tribes acted as siblings to each other.

Most sibling rivalry is fueled by a hidden mindset of scarcity. If Sean got more Lucky Charms than me, we might run out of Lucky Charms, and I wouldn't be able to get any more, and they might have stopped making Lucky Charms, and then I wouldn't ever be able to have them again, and it would all be Sean's fault.

Get the point? Sibling rivalry is all about looking out for numero uno.

I only have one brother, and we experienced this growing up. Can you imagine twelve?

Now, imagine that you are the nation of Israel, a tribe among tribes, but you're smaller and less established than all the other tribes around you, and you're just trying to survive in the world.

Scarcity. Survival. Justice (for me). These are the motivators that fuel sibling rivalry and tribal warfare. Build that into the fabric of an ancient religion, and you get all sorts of ideas about a God who is going to punish everyone but you, everyone who is not like you, and everyone who has ever done anything mean to you.

Someone's gonna pay.

This is how tribes think. This is how children think. But this is not how healthy parents think. And I'm pretty sure this is not how God thinks.

Isn't it interesting how this way of thinking has persevered throughout history, all the way to the present? We still have this insatiable hunger for justice, and it actually works against our father's grace.

The opposite of the scarcity mindset is *abundance*. There is enough to go around. I don't need my sibling to get a spanking for me to move up in the pecking order. In a culture of abundance, there is no pecking order. There's no need for one.

Can you imagine experiencing the kind of love that frees you from the need to compete, to compare or prove yourself? Can you imagine a spirituality that is spacious enough for you and everyone around you to be yourself?

GENEROSITY

It reminds me of a parable Jesus told about laborers in a vineyard in Matthew 20. At 9 a.m., a land owner hired some men to work in his vineyard and agreed to pay them a normal day's wages. At 5 p.m., the job wasn't quite done, so he found some more laborers and agreed to pay them the same amount to work the last part of the day.

The original laborers, who had been working all day, were furious, but the master told them to take their pay and go, as he was free to pay anyone any amount he wished. Before the parable ends, the master asks a haunting question of the angry men.

"Are you envious because I'm generous?"

Are we okay with God being generous to other people? What if he forgives someone you can't stand? What if you show up to the wedding feast in the age to come, and across the table from you is someone who wronged you or someone you were raised to hate or someone who believed differently than you?

Are you okay with your father's generosity? His extravagant

love? His wasteful grace?

When the music starts and the beat drops and all the unexpected prodigals hit the dance floor, will you join them, or will you be standing in the parking lot with your arms crossed, unwilling to share in your father's kindness?

CHAPTER THREE

. . . .

CLOSE

When I was a kid, I used to get scared in the middle of
the night. When I was really young, I would creep into my
parents' room and ask if I could sleep with them. By the time
I was in elementary school, I didn't want to disturb them,
so I would tiptoe down the hall and lay down outside their
bedroom door. I could hear my dad snoring through the wall,
so I knew everything was okay.

As I got a little older, maybe eight or nine, if I got scared at
night, I would sit in the entrance to my bedroom with the
hall light on.

One particular night, I slept sprawled out in my bedroom
doorway, half of my little body in my room, the other half in
the hall! For some reason, that seemed like a better option
than just staying in bed.

As the years passed, this common childhood fear of being alone at night faded. When I was getting ready to start high school, my parents let me move down to our unfinished basement.

It had cement walls plastered with posters of surfers and my favorite bands, tattered rugs covering the bare floor, a drum set, a Marshall JCM 800 half stack (that's a type of guitar amp that makes for really loud punk music), surfboards propped up against the walls, a bench press, and a Sony PlayStation (yeah, the original). It was pretty sweet, and it quickly became the place for my friends and I to hang out after school, lift weights, play music, and tell inappropriate jokes.

OTHER AIRPLANES

My little brother, Sean, had the same nighttime fears growing up but with one difference: He would often sleepwalk when he had a bad dream.

One night shortly after moving into my new basement apartment, I awoke to see Sean's silhouette in the doorway staring blankly at me, all *Children of the Corn* style.

Startled, I lunged out of my sheets. "Sean, what's wrong?"

"I'm scared," he replied.

"What are you scared of?"

"Other airplanes."

Clearly, we were having a different kind of conversation than I expected.

I realized he was still asleep, so I walked him back up to his bedroom. I was just glad he wasn't having a dream that involved axes or butcher knives! To this day, he still has no recollection of that night. I slept with one eye open for the rest of my teen years.

I'm not sure what I was afraid of all those years. Monsters under the bed? Something happening to my parents? Or maybe that they wouldn't be there when I woke up.

Kirby grew up with a strong church background, so she was always afraid that her family would get raptured in the night, and she would be *left behind*!

I saw a *Dennis the Menace* movie when I was young that featured the actor Christopher Lloyd (yes, Doc from *Back To The Future*) as a strange, nomadic, homeless man who kidnaps Dennis. The movie was a family comedy, but I used to have nightmares about that guy coming to get me!

I know now that these fears are common in children. As we

grow older, healthy adults learn how to feel safe and secure in their home, no longer anxious about the unknown.

PRESENCE

I realize, though, that these childhood anxieties can linger in the way we think about God. We have a tendency to think of him in terms of being either close or distant. When we pray, we plead with him to come near to us, not realizing that he is already here. We sing songs about it. I've written songs about it!

In our own adult way, we still lose sleep at night, worried that we might be alone in this big, empty universe without God snoring down the hall.

We may think of God as close one moment and distant the next, but the Bible paints a very different picture of his proximity to us, a picture of abiding closeness.

King David articulates this reality beautifully in Psalm 139.

> Where can I go from your Spirit? Where can I flee from your presence? If I go up to the heavens, you are there; if I make my bed in the depths, you are there. If I rise on the wings of the dawn, if I settle on the far side of the sea, even there your hand will guide me, your right hand will hold me fast. If I say, 'Surely the darkness will hide me and the

light become night around me,' even the darkness
will not be dark to you; the night will shine like
the day, for darkness is as light to you.

Earlier in the passage, David remarks that God is "intimately acquainted" with all of his ways and that God knows everything about him. The good, the bad, and the ugly. The Hebrew word for *know* used here is similar to the Greek word, *ginosko*, which we talked about earlier. In this case, it's *yada*. It speaks of intimate, even sexual, knowledge.

Later on in that psalm, David says that God's thoughts for him outnumber the stars in the sky and the sand on the shore.

This passage speaks to us about God's intimate knowledge of us, his inescapable presence with us, and his incomparable love for us.

It reveals a God who is so big and so present that there is not a single location in the universe (physically, emotionally, spiritually, or mentally) where he is not present. The Hebrew word for *depths* used in this passage is *sheol*, which is often translated as "hell" or "the grave."

Even if we go to the lowest possible place, David says, God is still with us. We couldn't get away from him if we tried.

What if we actually believed that God, knowing every detail about us, loves us completely and is always with us? That might just change our lives.

I love the Hebrew word for *presence* used in Psalm 139. It's the word *paniym,* and it is often translated as "face." It's as if David is saying, "No matter which way I turn, your face is always facing me. I can climb to the top of a mountain, I can descend to the lowest valley, I can get up early one morning and cross the sea, and your face is still shining on me.

I can get on a rocket ship and fly to Mars, and as soon as I touch down on the red planet, there you are, waiting for me with Matt Damon digging in the sand. I can even go down to the grave, to *sheol,* to the place of no return, and there you are."

What if I told you that you have never lived a day of your life without God's face shining upon you? That you have never met a person, nor will you ever meet a person, who has ever lived a single moment without God's face shining upon them?

His orientation toward us is love, and his presence is inescapable. Maybe you've been told that the Bible is all about the distance that exists between God and us, but Psalm 139 seems to tell us that the distance is primarily in our heads and that God is closer than we think.

THE MOVE

As a pastor, I talk to and pray with a lot of people who are making big life decisions and are concerned about making the wrong choice, of stepping "out of God's will." Have you ever heard anyone say something like that? Have you ever said something like that? I know I have.

Several years ago, Kirby and I were living in Columbus, Georgia (a city about an hour and a half south of Atlanta), leading a college and young adult ministry that we loved. We helped start the ministry with our dear friends, Grant and Krissy, and then we had the honor of taking it over a few years later. All in all, we led that ministry for five and a half years. During that time, God gave us a heart for the city of Columbus. I truly felt like it was "my city." I prayed for that city. I fasted for it. I received vision from God on behalf of it.

Then one day, an opportunity came to move to Atlanta and help lead a church called Grace Midtown with a group of my longtime friends. Kirby and I hadn't been looking to move or leave our ministry. We were perfectly content, even comfortable! We had just bought our first house, settled into some good family rhythms, and were really happy, but we couldn't shake the thought that maybe God had something more for us in Atlanta.

We took a few months to pray about it, and we even brought

our boss, Pastor Paul, into the conversation. He agreed to pray for us during those few months and was a constant source of encouragement and support. When we finally decided to leave Columbus for Atlanta and met with Pastor Paul to break the news, he told us that God had already tipped him off, and he and the church sent us out in love and confidence.

It was such a healthy transition, free of drama and hurt feelings. We could really feel God in the process.

But we still had lots of loose ends to tie up. We had to sell our house during an economic downturn and move to a new city with a much higher cost of living. We knew that *if God was in it*, he would take care of us.

The next few months were some of the most anxiety-ridden of our lives.

Over and over again, I prayed, "God, is this the right decision?" even after the decision had been made. I had never been so unsure of anything!

During those months, I was reading the Genesis account of Abraham's life. At one point when Abraham was having a hard time continuing to believe God and his promises, "God took him outside and said, 'Look up at the heavens and count the stars—if indeed you can count them.' Then he said to him, 'So shall your offspring be.'"

Over and over throughout that season of our lives, I felt God lead me outside and whisper, "Go count the stars," and I would remember how much bigger his plans are for our lives than we can possibly fathom.

FEED MY SHEEP

Up to that point in my life and ministry, whenever I was faced with a new opportunity or position, I sensed God telling me whether or not *he wanted me* to take it. When I was twenty years old and was offered a job as a youth pastor, I didn't want to take it (I was already leading worship at another church and had my own plans for music and ministry), but God impressed his desire for me to step into that position so clearly that I couldn't refuse.

One night, I drove out to that church property in the middle of the night to pray about the decision and heard that still, small voice speak to my heart.

"Feed my sheep."

"There are plenty of sheep where I am right now!" I shouted back. (Picture a shaggy-headed twenty-year-old pacing back and forth in a dark parking lot!)

"Feed my sheep."

"If you *really* want me to do this, I will."

"Feed my sheep."

"Are you going to take *everything* from me?!" I shouted as I tore my shirt. (I guess I was being a little dramatic.)

I had no idea at the time that those years spent as a youth pastor in that old United Methodist church would *form* me as a man and as a leader, that I would fall in love with those students and have the privilege of watching many of them begin a dynamic relationship with God, and that Kirby and I would learn what it looked like to do ministry together as a couple.

Fast-forward eight years, a few different ministries and churches later, and I found myself waiting for God to tell me *what he wanted me to do*. I kept expecting the wrestling match from those early days, but Kirby and I sensed he was telling us to do *whatever we wanted to do*. Maybe this is what the dynamics of a growing relationship with God are like. Just because he did it one way then doesn't mean he will do it the same way in the future.

I never realized that doing what we want can be a lot more difficult than doing what we're told.

We knew that if we were honest, we wanted to go to Atlanta to be a part of this new church with our friends and to embark on a new adventure. I kept thinking that if my life was a book, I wanted to be able to include that next chapter when I told people about it in my old age.

During the transition, people at our old church kept saying things like, "We'll miss you, but If God is making you go, you have to."

I would just smile nervously, not wanting to admit that God wasn't *making* us do anything. We were going, because we wanted to go, and God was freeing us to make that choice.

I knew that God wanted to lead us into so much more, but I was still scared of making the wrong decision.

I didn't want to admit it at the time, but I had a wrong belief about God. I was afraid that if I made a life decision that didn't line up with his "will" for my life (whatever that was), he would drop me like a bad habit, or at least remove his hand of provision and blessing.

Over those few months, between February and July of 2013, I turned the sale of our house into the litmus test of whether or not we were "in God's will." If we sold the house, didn't lose too much money, and made it to Atlanta in one piece, God was *with us*. If we were foreclosed on, lost everything, and were left destitute, we had clearly made a mistake.

TORNADOS

I'm pretty sure I had at least one or two panic attacks during
that time. You know, when you feel like a baby black hole
is forming in the center of your chest and is about to suck
everything within a five-foot radius into oblivion.

Oh, I'm the only one?

Kirby would wake up in the middle of the night with the
sensation that she was falling and couldn't catch herself, kind
of like that Leonardo DiCaprio movie about dreams. She also
had recurring nightmares about tornados blowing through
town and sweeping us away.

One morning after Kirby had suffered through another one
of those dreams, a friend of mine, whom I consider to be very
"prophetic" (someone who hears from God better than most)
texted me and said, "Hey, tell Kirby not to worry about the
tornados. Clear skies on the horizon for you guys."

We hadn't told anyone about her dreams! Time after time,
God continued to speak to us through the scriptures and
through our community, saying that we were on the right
track, that he was with us, that we didn't have to worry. But
we still struggled to gain peace.

For years, I had heard preachers use the idea of a "peace barometer" or "peace compass" when making big decisions. "If you have peace, God is in it. If you don't have peace, turn back." That all sounds like great advice, but in this circumstance, we believed we were making the right decision, but we didn't *feel* "peace" very often. It arrived in certain moments, but it was hard to hold onto. Like trying to grab a handful of smoke or retrieving a hasty text message after hitting "send," peace felt just beyond our reach. I realize now that we shouldn't spiritualize our feelings of anxiety or insecurity or areas where we may be unhealthy or immature.

Sometimes a "feeling" is just that, a feeling.

We started our ministry in Atlanta with our house in Columbus still on the market. Friends and church members in our new community were generous enough to let us stay with them, since we couldn't afford our old mortgage as well as rent for a new place. Matt and Margaret, our good friends and lead pastors at Grace Midtown, went on a sabbatical that summer, so we were able to stay in their house for a few months, too.

After four months of staying with friends and driving back and forth to Columbus to mow the lawn and flush the toilets, we ended up selling our house in July with a closing date during the last week of the summer, just before shifting into a busy fall schedule. I couldn't have come up with better timing for the whole thing if I had written the story myself!

Selling that house marked the end of a difficult transition in our lives, but looking back, I realize the only real hardship we experienced was in the form of our own anxiety and worry. At one point in the middle of the transition, I felt God speak to me, "You're going to be just fine, Rob. That's not in question. The only question is, 'When this is all over, will you have enjoyed yourself?'"

THE EMBRACE

One day, after being in Atlanta for a few months, during a staff prayer time in the office, my friend, Drew (also very prophetic), leaned over to me and said, "Hey, Rob, I've got this picture of you in my head. I see God reaching out to embrace you, but every time he extends his hand, you wince, like he's going to hit you. Like someone who has been in an abusive relationship or something."

Wow. Those words landed like a ton of bricks. He was right! I was afraid of God. I was afraid, because for the first time in a long time, Kirby and I were making a decision based on what we wanted. I felt so guilty, so selfish, even though we felt like God *told us* to do just that!

Somewhere beneath the surface in my subconscious, I thought I had forfeited God's good intentions toward me by choosing something that I would enjoy. I was so used to doing what I was told, obeying orders, that this new scenario seemed too good to be true. Surely God would take it away from me or punish me in some way.

I had struggled for months leading up to that moment to *feel* God's presence the way I had in the past. I was afraid he was mad at me, so I kept my distance. I was worried that if I heard him speak, he would tell me I had screwed up, so I avoided the conversation.

I didn't realize at the time that even if I had made the wrong decision, God would not have withdrawn his presence from me. I didn't know that even if, in seeking to obey God, I had "stepped off the path" (if that's even how it works!), he would have been right there waiting to catch me and extend his love to me.

What's more, I'm pretty sure that even if I had disobeyed him intentionally, he would have still been there, waiting for me to look up and catch his eye so he could remind me again that he loves me and that it's all going to be okay.

I know a lot of people who were raised to think that God's presence is something that comes and goes, that we can essentially *summon* him and *keep* him around by praying the right prayers and thinking the right thoughts and saying the right words and doing the right things. Fear is so easily instilled in us regarding our connection with the creator, a fragility to this eternal bond with the immortal one.

I have friends who, while growing up, thought that if they stubbed their toe, said a cuss word, and then were hit by a bus, their eternal destiny would be jeopardized by that moment of "unrepentant sin." As if their salvation was something that could be lost like a set of car keys or a wadded up receipt.

WITHIN REACH

I love Paul's words in Acts 17 when addressing a group of people in Athens, who were possibly further removed from his religious and cultural context than anyone else in the New Testament.

> "The God who made the world and everything in it is the Lord of heaven and earth and does not live in temples built by hands. And he is not served by human hands, as if he needed anything, because he himself gives all people life and breath and everything else. From one man, he made every nation, that they should inhabit the whole earth and he determined the times set for them and the exact places where they should live. God did this so that people would seek him and perhaps reach out for him and find him, though *he is not far from each one of us.* 'For in him we live and move and have our being.' As some of

your own poets have said, 'We are his offspring.'"

He is not far from us! In him we live and move and have our being!

The idea that God could be distant from us is just that, an idea. The reality is constant, uninterrupted closeness.

In his celebrated book about contemplative prayer, *Into The Silent Land*, Martin Laird argues that separation from God is an illusion. He memorably declares, "Union with God is not something that needs to be acquired, but realized."

For so long, I thought I had to reach and grasp in order to acquire and maintain my connection with God. I knew that it was given freely, but the responsibility of maintaining it seemed like it was entirely on my shoulders. When viewed this way, this precious union is something that can be threatened by our human weakness and frailty. I didn't realize that intimacy with God was something I was falling into rather than climbing up to obtain.

If you are in Christ, then you *are* one with God. You don't have to worry about that. Now, don't hear me wrong. I'm sure some readers are thinking of Paul's words in Romans 6, "Shall we go on sinning so that grace may increase?"

Of course I'm not advocating for a lack of self-control or

endorsing what Dietrich Bonhoeffer referred to as "cheap grace." I am simply suggesting that we, like Paul says in 1 Corinthians 13, "Put childish ways behind us" and let go of our adolescent anxieties that God might disappear in the night.

We don't have to fear losing our connection with God. By grace it is initiated, and by grace it is maintained.

FEAR OR LOVE

So many followers of Jesus are bound up by fear in the way they live and seek the kingdom of God. Fear is a great motivator—it gets results! But it's not the way of Jesus.

The beloved disciple wrote in 1 John 4,

> God is love. Whoever lives in love lives in God, and God in him or her. In this way, love is made complete among us so that we will have confidence on the day of judgment, because in this world we are like him. There is no fear in love. But perfect love drives out fear, because fear has to do with punishment. The one who fears is not made perfect in love.

Do you see how John speaks to the tension between fear and the confidence produced by love?

Fear is a great motivator, but love is better. Governments can use fear to get their people to do what they want. The God of the universe does not work that way. God uses love, because *God is love*. And his love gives us confidence as we navigate the twists and turns in the road of life.

Jesus comes not condemning the world but condemning the accuser!

He "cancelled the written code, with its regulations, that was against us and that stood opposed to us; he took it away, nailing it to the cross. And having disarmed the powers and authorities, he made a public spectacle of them, triumphing over them by the cross."

In my eleventh grade English class, we read Jonathan Edwards' legendary sermon, *Sinners In The Hands Of An Angry God*. As we read his warnings and threats of hellfire and brimstone, my classmates shuddered at the thought of God's anger toward them. The imagery of the following passage has stayed with me for the past thirteen years:

> The God that holds you over the pit of hell,
> much as one holds a spider, or some loathsome
> insect over the fire, abhors you, and is dreadfully
> provoked: his wrath towards you burns like fire;
> he looks upon you as worthy of nothing else,
> but to be cast into the fire; he is of purer eyes
> than to bear to have you in his sight; you are ten

thousand times more abominable in his eyes,
than the most hateful venomous serpent is in
ours.

Those words may have been useful in prompting the First Great Awakening, but (and I mean no disrespect to Edwards) they do not reflect the heart of God toward his creation.

I have news for you: God is not angry with you. He is not waiting for you to screw up. He is not dangling you like a spider on a spindly web over the fires of hell, longing to cast you out of his sight.

The longing of his heart is to embrace you. To pull you close. To save you from your own destructive tendencies.

He is not holding your past mistakes against you.

His orientation toward you is love.

Fear has to do with punishment. As long as we are expecting punishment, we will never lower our defenses and relax into intimacy with God. As long as we think union with God is something we have to obtain and maintain with our good behavior, we will never truly realize that union.

God has extended his hand toward us not to strike us but to embrace us.

What would it look like if you began viewing God as completely available? Completely loving? Completely compassionate?

Not distant.

Close.

This is the gospel of Jesus.

The good news.

Mark 1 says, "Jesus went into Galilee, proclaiming the good news of God. 'The time has come,' he said. 'The kingdom of God is near. Repent and believe the good news!'"

The kingdom is near (or at hand).

Within reach.

Close.

By the way, that word, *repent*, probably doesn't mean what you think. We're used to seeing it dripping down sandwich board signs on street corners or hearing it shouted by angry evangelists.

We think it means something like, "Feel really, really bad

about all the stuff you've done, and do better!"

The word *repent* is actually the Greek word *metanoeō,* and it means "to change your mind."

That's it. Change your mind. Change your mind about God. About yourself. About the world. Trade up your understanding.

The good news is that God is nearby, and all you have to do to experience him is think differently. Just receive it. Just "accept that you are accepted."

What if you could let go of fear?

What if you could let go of anxiety?

What if you could fall into love and receive from the God who is impossibly and inescapably . . .

Close?

CHAPTER FOUR

IMAGE

WHO DO YOU REMIND ME OF?

When I was in high school, my buddies and I became friends
with a youth pastor in his early twenties named Johnny B.

One day, Johnny B told us about an event he was hosting
at his church, and he wanted us to invite anyone from our
school who didn't know Jesus.

It just so happened that I had been in a conversation with a
girl (we'll call her Laura) in my gym class who confessed to
me that she didn't really have a relationship with God. She
told me she used to go to church with some friends, but it
had been a long time, and she felt far from God. Excitedly, I
invited her to come out to Johnny B's event.

When I showed up with my friends at the church that Friday night, Laura was there! I was thrilled that God might do something in her life and that I might have played a role in it by inviting her out.

When the event ended, she seemed genuinely moved. As everyone was walking out to the parking lot, Laura asked me if she could have a ride home.

"Of course." I was thrilled to hear what she thought about the event.

In the car, Laura had a confession to make. "My parents are Catholic, and they're really conservative, and I don't think they would understand why I would want to come out to an event like this. So I told them you were taking me out on a date."

"Uh . . ."

"They're very traditional," she continued, "And they want to meet you."

"Umm . . ."

"They have gifts for you."

"Ummm . . ."

"And they don't speak English."

I guess I should mention that Laura's parents had immigrated from Latin America before she was born.

"Sounds great," I said. Gulp. What the heck had I gotten myself into?

When we pulled up to Laura's house, she added, "I have to warn you, my little brothers are crazy."

"Perfect."

As we approached the door, Laura's parents met us outside, while her brothers wrestled in the yard. Her parents hugged my neck and began handing me boxes of chocolates and other treats. Laura and her parents exchanged a few comments in Spanish while I stood there awkwardly, wishing I had stayed awake in Spanish class.

After a couple of minutes, her mom leaned in and stared intently at my face and said something that I couldn't understand. Then everyone burst into laughter.

I turned to Laura. "What did she say?"

"She said you look like Chuck Norris!"

Now, let me assure you, I have never been accused of looking like Chuck Norris in my entire life. I don't have red hair, I can't grow an impressive beard, I don't own cowboy boots, my tears can't cure cancer, I have absolutely no martial arts skills (despite the aforementioned *Robby Kaple's Secret Sword of the Ninja Club*), and I have never sold home exercise equipment on television.

At that moment, Laura's two little brothers started running in circles around me chanting, "Chuck! Chuck! Chuck! Chuck!"

I couldn't have made up that story if I tried.

What do people say when they look at you? They might say you have your mom's eyes or your dad's hair or your grandpa's handyman skills or that you look like Chuck Norris. What does God say when he looks at you?

VERY GOOD

When we read the creation poem at the beginning of Genesis, we see that God created Adam and Eve, the first humans (the word *Adam* actually means "man" or "mankind") in his own *image* or likeness. God gazed at all he had made, at the man and the woman placed together in the garden, and said it was "very good."

I don't know what you've heard about humanity or creation or original sin, but there was a day when God looked at humanity and said it was very good.

In his book, *Waking the Dead*, John Eldredge says, "We've heard a bit about original sin, but not nearly enough about original glory, which comes before sin and is deeper to our nature. We were crowned with glory and honor."

In the beginning . . .

It was good.

We were good.

We were made to be like God. In fact, Adam and Eve's placement in the garden came with a job description. They were to rule over the planet. Dallas Willard calls this God's "creation covenant," saying that having something to rule over or to steward is part of what makes us human.

Of everything God created—animals, oceans, atoms, and angels—we were the only ones made in his image. We resemble him in distinct ways, and we were made to partner with him in his creative activity.

We all know what happened next.

Serpent.

Tree.

Sin.

Shame.

Pain.

Death.

The way it all went down is interesting though. In the center
of the garden were two trees—the tree of life and the tree of
the knowledge of good and evil. One would sustain, the other
destroy.

The serpent came to Eve and drew her attention to the tree of
the knowledge of good and evil and told her if she ate from it,
she would become *like* God.

Did you catch that? The enemy tricked her by tempting her
with something she *already possessed.*

She and Adam were *already* like God, made in his image,
but they gave in to the lie that God was holding out on them.
Almost all temptation comes in the form of a lie that suggests
what God has said is not true.

So, Adam and Eve ate from the tree of the knowledge of good
and evil, and immediately, their eyes were opened, and they
were able to make judgments about what was good, what was
bad, what was right, and what was wrong. Up to this point,

they had no need for that vocabulary or that way of thinking, because they didn't view the world around them in those terms.

"The man has now become like one of us, knowing good and evil," God said to himself after seeing what had happened. "He must not be allowed to reach out his hand and take also from the tree of life and eat, and live forever" (Genesis 3:22). It appears that God made the difficult decision not to allow Adam and Eve to live forever in their new state, perhaps because they could not steward creation properly into eternity with this propensity to critique the world and each other.

NAKED AND AFRAID

After eating the fruit, "Both of their eyes were opened," and they began to make judgments about the things around them. I think it's interesting that the first thing Adam and Eve make any sort of judgment about is themselves. They look down and at each other and realize they are naked, and for the first time in human history, they feel shame.

Some would argue that this ability to judge between good and bad is too great a burden for us to bear, a weight that humanity was never meant to carry. Through all of scripture runs a narrative of God teaching us how to view the world aright, free from the need to judge each other, free from the shame of not being what we think we should be, free from the worldly system of measuring human worth and value.

Paul puts it this way in 2 Corinthians 5:16: "So from now on we regard no one from a worldly point of view. Though we once regarded Christ in this way, we do so no longer."

Think about the way we qualify ourselves and the people around us.

Fat.
Skinny.
Intelligent.
Dumb.
Ugly.
Attractive.
Talented.
Rich.
Poor.
Successful.
Lazy.

We have all eaten of this tree and have become our own harshest critics, and in doing so have created our own *Great Commandment*: "Judge your neighbor as yourself."

We can't love anyone until we love ourselves, and that act becomes nearly impossible as long as we are still eating that ancient fruit.

Sadly, most major religions are built on eating of the tree of the knowledge of good and evil.

Little in this world is as destructive as self-hatred. When we look at ourselves and condemn what God has called "very good," we build a blockade against the Spirit's affirming, life-giving voice. Conversely, little is more freeing in this world than meeting someone who actually loves him or herself.

Have you ever met someone like that? Someone who truly has nothing to prove? I'm not talking about that cocky, false confidence that peacocks around and puffs itself up. I'm talking about the quiet self-assurance that doesn't mind serving others or lifting other people up, because it actually doesn't have anything to gain or lose.

True contentment.

MASKS

A lot of literature has come out over the past few years about the *false self*. The big idea is that, at some point in every person's childhood, they experience fear, pain, rejection, or some sort of instability that caused them to reevaluate their own value and worth. The process is subconscious but very real.

Usually, it goes something like this: Instability occurs. We feel insecure. We fear we won't be accepted by our peers (think first day of middle school). So we construct a version of ourselves that we think will be accepted: the jock, the bully, the cheerleader, the smart girl.

The false self is not necessarily bad or evil. It is merely incomplete. It's an exaggeration of our actual gifts and personality traits. The parts of ourselves that we actually like and that we think others will accept as well. But it becomes a mask, a shield, keeping everyone at a safe distance from our heart.

At the core of every person is a fear that if I let the people around me see who I really am, if I let them see my heart, my dreams, my fears, my passions, and my desires, they will reject me. So I'll just present a version of myself that I think the world will embrace.

The danger is the false self can actually do pretty well in the world. The false self can win awards and get promotions and find a spouse and acquire a lot of Instagram followers.

But being accepted and embraced for the mask you're wearing is perhaps the loneliest existence possible.

I have a haunting memory from my freshman year of high school. I was standing at the front of my English class. I don't remember if I was giving a presentation or if it was as class was ending and I had everyone's attention. Either way, I was telling a funny story, and I had the whole class laughing. People had tears running down their faces. They loved it. They loved me.

In that moment, I thought, "I can do this. I can be *the funny guy.*"

You remember what it was like to be fifteen. "Identity Crisis" was your middle name. Everyone was looking for a group, a clique. Everyone was figuring out their role in their circle of friends. After a semester and a half of trying to stay afloat amidst the wreckage of teen angst, I had found a life raft.

The funny guy.

What no one around me knew was that earlier that semester, I had decided to tell a girl that I liked how I felt about her. But I waited too long, and she started dating one of my friends.

Rejection.

I also tried out for my high school's soccer team. I played soccer throughout my adolescence and teen years, and I was pretty good, but I entered high school at 6 feet tall and 145 pounds, and the guys on the varsity team were big. The coach told me to gain some weight and try again next year.

Rejection.

I had started playing guitar earlier that year and had written a few songs in my basement bedroom. I had never really sung before though, so I was scared of letting anyone hear my voice.

Rejection (or at least the fear of it).

But humor, I could do that. Maybe I could be the best at it. I could win at making people laugh. And I did. Literally.

Three years later, I was elected "funniest" for our senior superlatives. I acted like it wasn't a big deal, but inside, I felt like I had won an Academy Award™.

I continued throughout college and into my twenties playing the role of the funny guy. That guy evolved, of course. I was also the preacher guy. The worship leader guy. The wise guy. The leadership guy.

At the core of it all was a desire to shine. To be special. To be impressive. I wanted to be the best at something. Anything.

It's taken me fifteen years to realize what happened that day in my freshman English class.

There's nothing wrong with being funny. It's part of who I am. It's a gift. A part of my personality. (If you haven't laughed out loud at some point while reading this book, I'll be offended.) But it became my mask.

My shield.
My salvation.

Thomas Merton refers to the false self as our personal plan for salvation. It's how we can be accepted. By the world. By ourselves. Ultimately, by God.

The reality is that behind the mask exists a real person who has already been accepted. A real person with intrinsic worth and dignity. A real person whom God has called "very good."

And God will stop at nothing to tear down our façade, remove our mask, and expose us to the world. Not to humiliate us but to honor us. Not so we can be rejected but embraced.

As Jonathan Martin has said, "God allows all our personas to crumble in order to make us into persons. It is terribly painful, but it is all grace."

BETTER NEWS

That's probably the hardest thing about following Jesus,

believing that who we really are is actually beautiful in God's sight. I'm not saying we don't all have our own mess that needs to be cleaned up or that sin is not a real thing. But we have all these terribly unhelpful Christian catchphrases that shape how we view ourselves and the rest of humanity.

"Love the sinner, hate the sin." (Read that in your best *church lady* voice.)

We can start to think of "sin" as a certain type of action that God says is bad. What if sin is anything that divides or alienates, anything that seeks to separate us from God, from each other, from ourselves? What if sin is not simply a behavior?

Behavior is a symptom. The real disease goes much deeper.

We're all stumbling around in the darkness, grasping for love, beauty, acceptance, significance, security, meaning, and worth, and it causes us to do some pretty messed-up stuff.

We've all heard preachers talk about the fact that God is so holy that he can't be in the presence of sin, and that if you've put your faith in Jesus, God doesn't see you when he looks at you. He sees Jesus. So you don't have to worry about him being angry with you, turning away from you or punishing you.

Martin Luther (who did some amazing stuff for the Church in his day) said that, in Christ, we are like "snow-covered dung." We're still disgusting and worthless, but at least Jesus gives us a sacred veneer that provides the appearance of holiness in the eyes of a just and wrathful God. But if he accidently steps on us, he's not gonna be happy about what's on his boot!

Is this the best description we can come up with to talk about the love of God? Is this the good news? "God hates you. You're disgusting. But he loves Jesus, so Jesus can trick God into thinking you're like him."

There's a story in the book of Genesis about a guy named Jacob. Jacob was a twin, the younger twin, to be exact. He was born clutching his brother Esau's heel. Throughout his life, Jacob struggled with Esau, struggled with his identity, and struggled with God.

Esau was a man's man. He loved to hunt. He was wild. He was also known for having thick, red hair all over his body. (I think I went to high school with a guy like that!)

When Jacob and Esau were grown, their father, Isaac, became weak, his eyes failed, and he approached the end of his life. It was the custom in those days for the father to bless his firstborn son before he died. When the time came, Jacob's mother told him to sneak into the tent and pretend to be his follicularly bountiful brother. He put on Esau's clothes, covered himself in goat skins, and rolled into his half-blind dad's room with a bowl of Jacob's favorite stew.

It was a weird idea, but the con worked. Jacob gained his father's blessing but lost his soul. Can you imagine? Blessing and acceptance only came when he was wearing a disguise. When he was pretending to be someone else. Using someone else's name.

Side note: How hairy was Esau if the goatskin disguise was an accurate portrayal of his forearms?

Years later, Jacob encountered a man in the middle of the night as he was crossing the river Jabbok. He wrestled with him all night until the man was willing to bless him. The man asked Jacob his name, and for the first time in his life, Jacob owned his true identity.

"My name is Jacob."

Just before the sun rose, the man blessed Jacob and gave him the name *Israel*, because he was one who struggled with God and with man.

This is one of the more peculiar accounts in the Old Testament, but it speaks deeply into our need for self-acceptance.

I would argue that a major point of the Jacob/Israel conversion story is to show us that God doesn't want our false self, our spiritual costume, or our holiness façade.

This is the root of Jesus' rebuke of the Pharisees, who only cleaned the outside of the dish but who were no better than whitewashed tombs, filled with dead men's bones.

When I was a young pastor, I remember hearing one of my contemporaries use a popular analogy to explain the work of the cross. It went something like this:

A man died and found himself in a courtroom before an angry judge. The judge rolled out a screen and a projector and made the man watch a film of his life. All of his failures and secret sins were laid bare before him. At the end of the film, just as the judge was about to drop the gavel, the courtroom doors burst open, and in walked Jesus, shouting, "Not so fast, Dad! This one's with me!"

John 3:16 is one of the most famous verses in the Bible. If you've watched any sort of nationally televised athletic event, you've probably seen a guy wearing a rainbow afro with the reference on his T-shirt. Most of us can probably quote some version of it.

What does it say? "For God was so disgusted with the world that he sent his son down in a hazmat suit to clean things up so he wouldn't have to destroy it."

No!

"For God so *loved* the world that he *gave* his only son."

Love

God loved us so much that he came to us.

The prophet, Isaiah, spoke of the Messiah who was to come and told us he would be called *Immanuel*, God with us.

CAN I BORROW YOUR HAND SANITIZER?

Jesus constantly offended the traditions of the self-righteous religious teachers. By the time he arrived on the scene, the Pharisees had added their own customs to the law's requirements. One of those customs was ceremonial hand washing. It was basically the equivalent of religious germaphobia.

At one point in the gospels, Jesus was questioned about why he and his disciples didn't participate in the over-the-top hand washing technique when they ate. He responded by telling them it's not what goes into a person that makes him or her unclean but what comes out of the heart.

Under the law, if a person touched a leper, that person became unclean. When Jesus touched a leper, the leper became clean. Adulterers were supposed to be killed by being bludgeoned with large stones. Jesus allowed them to pour perfume on him and wash his feet with their tears.

The incarnation of Jesus was always meant to be more than a *rescue*. Jesus is a *revelation*. He shows us what God is really like and how humanity was always meant to live.

The second Adam came to restore to humanity the identity and the vocation that the first Adam lost.

"Be fruitful and multiply."

"Go to the ends of the earth."

"Make disciples of all nations."

"Extend the dominion of the kingdom of the heavens."

One promise Jesus makes to "those who overcome" in the book of Revelation is that we will come and sit on his throne with him. To rule and to reign! That has always been the invitation.

We are still called to carry the image of God. Long before your sin and shame, there was glory.

This can be hard to see sometimes. We are so aware of humanity's brokenness. We turn on the news or check our social media feeds, and we're bombarded with another shooting.

Another massacre.

Another young man killed in police custody.

Embezzlement.

Scandal.

Oppression.

We also face the ache of discontentment in our own lives.

Back to work.

Back to class.

Pay the bills.

Wash it all down with an evening of salty take-out and a Netflix binge. We're plagued by the lingering thought that there must be something more. Haunted by the ghost of what could have been, what was always meant to be, God's original intent for humanity.

VOCATION

Following Jesus has to amount to more than simply adopting new systems of sin management and behavior modification. Surely the Son of Man did not come just to get us to believe the right stuff.

In fact, Jesus' promise was for an abundant life. The eternal kind of life now. A life rich with purpose and adventure, mystery and beauty. A life of partnership with the Creator in his creation.

God is still creating, and he's looking for people who want to be part of it. He's still writing the story, and he's inviting us to play along.

Every vocation is holy. Entire streams of the Christian faith exist just to get as many people as possible to become fully funded overseas missionaries or pastors at local churches (or at least to give a lot of money to support those ministries!). Of course I believe in sending missionaries and raising up pastors. I'm a pastor at a local church, and I have a sense of calling to vocational ministry, so I want to affirm that in others who have a similar calling. But a groundswell is growing across every sector of society. Jesus followers are waking up to the beauty and the holiness of their diverse vocations.

One woman at our church is a midwife. She is so passionate about her work! One day as she was telling me about how she gets to impact and empower women as they engage with the birthing process, tears rolled down her face. She's doing what she was born to do, and it's holy.

Another friend of mine owns a successful branding company in Atlanta. He's kind of a freakish combination of creativity and business savvy. He's always gathering people together and inspiring them and doodling pictures and innovating how he runs his business. It's a holy thing.

Another one of my friends works with special needs children. She loves it. She has a supernatural capacity for patience and gentleness. She walks in empathy with these children in ways that few people can. God created her with a unique passion to serve "the least of these," those who can't serve themselves, and it is a sacred calling.

My wife is an amazing singer. Seriously, her voice does something to people when they hear it. Whether she's leading worship or humming along to something on the radio, whenever she opens her mouth, peace enters the room. So many of our friends with infants and young children have told us that when their kids are having a rough time getting to sleep, they will throw on one of her songs, and suddenly everything is right in the world.

When we started dating, we used to lead worship together all the time. After a service, people would approach us and say something like, "We always love it when you guys sing. Rob, you're great and everything, but Kirby! I mean, wow!" I get it. When Kirby sings, she is living her calling, reflecting God's beauty, and taking hold of the holy vocation of cultivating the garden God has given her.

Every person who has ever lived was created in God's image. This is why human life is so precious. This is why something inside us breaks when we hear about someone dying before their time. This is why the taking of another person's life is unacceptable to us and to God, no matter who the person is. It's not just the born-again believer whose life is valuable. Murder is evil, because it is the destruction of a life crafted in the image of God.

In the same way, we are able to see this glory peek through even in people who we may not think of as Jesus followers. Have you ever heard people talk about Michael Jackson's talent as a singer and performer? "It's like he was anointed to do what he did," a friend of mine expressed in one conversation.

Or think about an entrepreneur like Steve Jobs. He brought so much innovation to the world of personal computers that he ended up impacting multiple other industries. Right now, I'm typing on a MacBook Pro, listening to music on my iPhone, and have used the Kindle app on my iPad to pull resources for this chapter. Tonight, I'm sure Kirby and I will stream one of our favorite shows from our Apple TV. Jobs was born to innovate and create, and regardless of what you may have heard about his character or his religious beliefs (neither of which I can speak of with any authority), his vocation was holy, and in one way or another, he reflected the glory of God.

HUMAN

That's the thing about imperfection. It's our imperfections that make us human. And it's our humanity that makes us spiritual.

I read a tweet from Eugene Peterson the other day that I just can't shake. (Yes, Eugene Peterson, the guy who wrote the Bible, has a Twitter account.) (I know, Eugene Peterson didn't actually write the Bible, but he paraphrased it into *The Message*, which is still pretty impressive.)

"We don't become more spiritual by becoming less human."

Isn't that what most of us are trying to do? Isn't that what so many of our church activities and religious practices and quiet times and worship services are doing for us?

De-humanizing.

If I can just detach from this wretched flesh and these worthless thoughts and my worldly job, then I might be able to ascend, to climb the mountain, to arrive at my destiny.

God doesn't love us and fill us and embolden us despite our humanity, but in the midst of it.

He created us with these bodies, and he intends to resurrect them so we can hold onto them for a while longer. In fact, Jesus shows us what it looks like when God wears the same skin we do.

He ate.
He drank.
He slept. He even took naps. (Hallelujah!)
He prayed.
He laughed.
He wept.

Have you ever thought about the fact that Jesus lived for thirty years before beginning his ministry? He didn't heal anyone or cast out any demons. He didn't multiply food or open blind eyes. He wasn't dying on a cross for the sins of the world. For thirty years, he just lived.

Jesus had a job. What? Yeah. He was a carpenter. It's not like he was working in the woodshop by day so he could pursue his real passion at night and on the weekend. He wasn't taking online classes or writing a screenplay. He just worked and hung out with friends and family and went to the synagogue. He was probably in a bowling league and played fantasy football.

If the "spiritual" part of his life was all that mattered, why didn't he start sooner? If it was only about dying for our sins, why not be more efficient? You know, in and out like a team of Navy SEALs. Jump out of the helicopter, swing through the window on a harness. On the cross, in the grave, resurrected before you can say "Steven Seagal."

For some reason, it was important for Jesus to live a normal life. It was important for God to become one of us. Blessed John Duns Scotus (what a name!), a twelfth-century Franciscan monk, argued that even if the fall had not taken place, the incarnation still would have.

What? Christ came to Earth for more than a rescue mission?

Part of being fully human means that Jesus faced all of the same temptations we face on a daily basis. Following Jesus doesn't mean despising our humanity but embracing it. God became a man, and in doing so redefined what it means to be human.

Every person you have ever met was crafted in the image of the almighty God.

C.S. Lewis puts it this way:

> The dullest and most uninteresting person you
> talk to may one day be a creature which, if you
> saw it now, you would be strongly tempted to
> worship, or else a horror and corruption such
> as you now meet if at all only in a nightmare . . .
> *There are no ordinary people. You have never*
> *talked to a mere mortal* . . . But it is immortals
> whom we joke with, work with, marry, snub,
> and exploit—Immortal horrors or everlasting
> splendors.

What does God see when he looks at you? Snow-covered
dung or a precious image-bearer, a child born of glory and
wonder?

What does the world see? Just another ordinary person or an
everlasting splendor?

Are you simply taking up space, punching the clock and
paying the bills, or are you carrying out the holy vocation of
cultivating God's created world?

What if your life is holy, not just because you are forgiven
and redeemed but because you are human?

CHAPTER FIVE

. . . .

MOVEMENT

I turned twenty-one years old in Jerusalem.

I had the amazing opportunity to go on a trip to Israel with the church I worked at when I was in college and celebrated my twenty-first birthday while I was there. Early that morning, we woke up in Jerusalem and drove down to Jericho and to the Dead Sea. We, like many other tourists and pilgrims, decided to go for a swim in the saltiest place on Earth.

It's true what they say. The Dead Sea is so salty that you can literally float on the surface. We were warned not to let any of the water get into our eyes or mouth, as it would burn and taste terrible. (I can testify to that; it's not pleasant.) The experience was surreal. We were like little human buoys bobbing on top of this giant desert lake.

As we got out of the water, I saw an elderly man in a Speedo (not kidding) giving people mud massages (also not kidding), so I thought, *How often do you turn twenty-one at the Dead Sea?* The mud at the Dead Sea is proven to have healing properties because of all the nutrients in it. So I threw caution to the wind and let this scantily clad stranger go to town.

After my birthday mud massage, I tried to walk away, but the man stopped me and said six words I will never forget: "My massage is not free, sir!" (Use your imagination with the accent.)

Realizing I had left my wallet on the bus, our tour guide gave the guy five bucks and hurried me along. We were in the middle of the desert, and I let a strange man in a Speedo rub mud all over me. I was young, a bit naïve, and I guess I thought he worked for the Dead Sea or something. But this was not Disneyworld, and there were no lines or ticket booths!

In the Old Testament, Ezekiel has a vision of a river coming out from under the threshold of the temple. It started at the altar and trickled out of the doorway, out the gate, and to the east. This river got deeper and wider as it moved further from the temple. It started out ankle deep and then went up to the knee, then the waist, and then it was deep enough to swim in, and Ezekiel found himself getting swept away by the current.

Trees began to grow along the side of the river, and they bore fruit in and out of season. Many different kinds of fish swam in the river. Eventually, the river met the Dead Sea and turned the salty water fresh, where it was able to support different kinds of life.

The Dead Sea is called the Dead Sea for a reason. It's so salty and stagnant that almost nothing can live in it.

MOVEMENTS AND MONUMENTS

You may not have had the opportunity to visit the Dead Sea, swim in it, or get a mud massage by a stranger in inappropriate swimwear, but I bet you've found yourself in some places that are a lot like the Dead Sea.

Maybe you grew up in a church, a denomination, a family, a town, or a school that was like the Dead Sea—a stagnant lake that hasn't had any fresh water flow into it in years, lacking vitality and life.

I don't want to be too hard on churches and denominations, because at some point in their history, they were probably a lot like the mighty river flowing from the temple. People would fish from their shores and swim in their depths. There was movement afoot.

That's the thing about movements. They have to keep moving . . . or they cease to be movements.

Far too often, our movements eventually become monuments.

Jesus promised in John 7 that if anyone came to him to drink, rivers of living water would flow from that person. He used similar language to describe himself and the working of the Spirit to the woman at the well in John 4.

The phrase "living water" used throughout the scriptures actually means "moving water."

In those days, that was what made a body of water "living" or "dead."

Movement.

A river is living. A pond is dead. That doesn't mean nothing can live in a pond, but if you put your foot in it, you're probably going to step on something squishy.

What made the Dead Sea teem with life in Ezekiel's dream was movement. What makes the Dead Sea remain dead is stagnancy.

Movement is crucial to life and vitality. If you took biology in your freshmen year of high school and remember anything besides dissecting a cat, you might remember being taught about the seven processes of life.

Movement
Respiration
Sensitivity
Growth
Reproduction
Excretion
Nutrition

If you need help remembering, just think of the acronym "Mrs. Gren."

Without movement, there is no life. Nothing alive remains still (even if it moves really slowly, like a snail or a sea anemone or your Great Aunt Yolanda). God is referred to as the *living* God, and God is always moving. So, to follow Jesus means to be on the move.

Always.

During their midnight conversation in John chapter 3, Jesus explains to Nicodemas that following the Spirit is like following the wind. You don't know where it's going or where it's coming from.

It is impossible for the Church to exist as God intended without movement. Sadly, many churches and ministries that started as movements have grown silent and still, void of motion, void of life.

The first-century church started out in motion. The day of Pentecost in Acts 2 acted as a sort of "Big Bang" for the body of Christ. Like our universe, God's kingdom has been expanding ever since.

Not only did the Church start out in motion, it was intended to remain in motion.

Throughout my twenties, I worked for several different churches within several different denominations, and I learned a lot about modern Church history. While on staff at one of those churches, I took a class on the history of that particular denomination. What I learned saddened me.

The story is familiar, because it is true of almost every major Protestant denomination. A few hundred years ago, a group of people experienced a powerful move of God. Converts were made, bodies were healed, missionaries were sent out, and churches were planted.

As the group grew, the necessary organizational structures and doctrinal statements and constitutions and bylaws were put in place.

All good things.

All necessary to sustain a growing movement.

Without organization, chaos ensues.

What saddened me was the realization that, a few hundred years later, those structures and doctrinal statements and constitutions and bylaws had become more important than the movement itself.

The means, like so many times before, had become the end.

Like I said, I don't want to be too hard on the Church. And don't try to guess which denomination I'm talking about, because I've worked in several of them, and the story goes about the same way every time.

The point is, it's easy to turn a movement into a monument.

Imagine if NASA never took another expedition into space but kept the organization going as a group of space shuttle enthusiasts.

Future generations of schoolchildren would learn about the rockets and engines and orbiters and air locks. They would take field trips to see a shuttle in person and marvel at the sheer size of the thing. Experts could give their entire lives to studying the types of materials used to build them and even the type of fuel used in the engines and never realize that the whole point of space shuttles (and NASA) was exploration of outer space.

It's easy to turn a vehicle into a destination. Making an end out of the means.

SNAKES ON A PLAIN (SEE WHAT I DID THERE?)

In 2 Kings 18, we read about Hezekiah, King of Judah. Hezekiah was a good king who did right in the eyes of the Lord. He removed the high places, smashed the sacred stones, and cut down the Asherah poles. These represented the various ways the Israelites worshiped false gods.

Hezekiah did one other thing to help get Israel back on track: He smashed the bronze snake that Moses had fashioned in the desert.

If you're not familiar with the bronze snake story, it originates in Numbers 21 and goes something like this: After being delivered from Pharaoh's army through the Red Sea, the Israelites grumbled against the Lord, so he sent venomous snakes that bit the people. Then God told Moses to make a snake out of bronze and lift it up in the air. Anyone who had been bitten could look upon the bronze snake and live.

I know, strange story.

My friend, Matt Reynolds, has made some fascinating observations about this story. Generations after fashioning the bronze snake in obedience to God, the Israelites had made it into an idol and began to worship it and burn incense to it.

How incredible is that? Something that God commanded to a previous generation had become an idol for a future generation.

This obscure story contains an important lesson for us. Obsession with what God said or did *yesterday* can actually impede our ability to be a part of what God is saying and doing *today*. I doubt any of us are in danger of worshiping a metal reptile, but history does tell us that we can easily miss out on what God is *doing* because we're so hung up on what he *did*.

Surely the people who are in the most danger of missing out on the next great move of God are those who were a part of the last one.

I'll let you take a second to chew on that last sentence. Seriously, read it again.

COUNTING THE COST

I think this is why so many people had a hard time following Jesus in his day. Their life was built around what God did hundreds of years before. To change, to pick up and follow what God was doing in the present, would mean letting go of everything they had known up to that point.

This is why Jesus was so stern with people when they were hesitant to follow him. He didn't beg. Often, he just walked away.

Take the rich young ruler, for instance. This man asked what he needed to do to inherit eternal life. Jesus told him to obey the commandments.

"I do!" the man replied.

Then Jesus told him to sell everything and follow him. The man couldn't do it, so he went away sad. And Jesus was fine with it.

Or take the guy who said he needed to bury his father before he followed Jesus.

"Let the dead bury their own dead."

Harsh.

Or what about when Jesus was in a crowded house teaching everyone who was following him. It says there were so many people that he couldn't even get away for a moment to eat, and his family thought he was crazy. When one of his disciples told him his mother and brothers had come to see him, he pointed to the people in the house and said, "These are my mother and brothers, those who do the will of God."

Jesus knew what it would cost to break from the old system, and he gave himself exclusively to those who were willing to pay that price.

GHOSTS, GHOULS, AND GOBLINS

It seems the more familiar we become with Jesus, the more susceptible we become to missing what he is doing.

During his ministry in Galilee, Jesus was constantly dragging his disciples out of their comfort zones. They would hop on a boat and cross over to the other side of the Sea of Galilee (that is to say, to the home of the people who were completely *other*).

One of those occasions followed the miraculous feeding of five thousand people. Jesus and his disciples were out in the countryside, and the crowds followed them out there to be touched by Jesus. He healed their diseases and cast demons out of people and taught them about the kingdom of God.

They had been out there so long that everyone was getting hungry, and there was not enough food for all of the people. What did Jesus do, send everyone home? Nope.

He took a few loaves of bread and a few small fish, divided them up in the hands of the disciples, and had them serve dinner to the crowd. Amazingly, there was enough food for everyone to eat their fill, and there were twelve basketfuls of leftovers.

That night, Jesus told the disciples to hop in the boat and go across without him. They set out on the sea but faced a killer storm in the middle of the night and struggled at the oars. Jesus, intending to pass by them (yep, that's what it says), walked out on the water where they were paddling.

I've always been intrigued by what happens next.

When they saw him, they thought he was a ghost, and they were terrified.

Really? A ghost? That was their first thought? This is quickly starting to sound like an episode of *Scooby-Doo* rather than a gospel account.

What strikes me about this story is that, in one afternoon, an incredible miracle could take place (the multiplication of a few fish and loaves to feed five thousand people) in the hands of the disciples, and later that evening, they could look at Jesus and not even recognize him.

I have to confess; I've been that disciple before. Not that I've ever busted out five thousand hamburgers at a football game or filled a shopping mall with broken pieces of an Auntie Anne's pretzel. (You know, the cinnamon kind. With the dip. I need to go to the mall.) But God has used me in one moment to minister to people in incredible ways, and in the next moment, I have failed to recognize Jesus in a strange and unfamiliar context.

Mark's gospel tells us the disciples didn't recognize Jesus because their hearts were hardened. When Jesus rebuked them, he asked if they had eyes that didn't see and ears that didn't hear.

Sobering isn't it?

You can have hands that work miracles but ears that aren't awake.

Maybe that's what Jesus meant when he said that many would come saying, "Lord, Lord, didn't we prophesy and cast out demons in your name?" And that he would reply, "I never knew you."

That word, *knew*. You guessed it, *ginosko*.

Few guarantees come with following Jesus, but here's one: Every now and then, Jesus will walk out on the water looking like a ghost.

You'll be tempted to be afraid, or you'll have all sorts of reasons why that's not actually Jesus.

However, I've discovered that each new revelation is also an invitation.

An invitation to step out on those waters. An invitation to follow Jesus into that new context. That new situation. To those new people. To that new place.

He's always moving.

SURF'S UP

I love surfing. I grew up just outside of Atlanta, Georgia, but for one brief, glorious year in middle school, my family and I lived in Orange County in Southern California. That's where I learned to surf. I became obsessed, and I still am. Now I only get to surf a few times a year, but each time I do, it's like fresh air in my lungs.

I love the feel of the ocean water on my skin. The colors of the sun on the horizon. The smell of the salty air. I even love the smell of a freshly waxed surfboard or a drying wetsuit.

I've found that the act of surfing has spoken profoundly into how I understand walking with God.

First of all, surfing is all about responding.

It's not like most other sports, where you are performing on a static surface. Surfing is about what the ocean is doing and responding to that.

When a group of surfers is sitting out in the water, they always face the horizon. Their backs are turned to the shore, where spectators and jobs and bills and highways reside. For this reason, surfing acts as a momentary respite from life's worries and responsibilities.

Surfers watch the horizon, because that's where the waves come from. It's hard to see a set of waves from a long way off. (Waves come in sets, by the way. Sometimes there are just one or two waves in a set, while at other times there may be six or eight. It all depends on the consistency and strength of the wind in the storm that generated the waves in the middle of the ocean.) But you can spot a potential set approaching by watching the horizon to see if the water rises momentarily.

Catching a wave is an interesting experience, too. Location and timing are the two key factors. As a wave approaches, you have to start paddling toward the shore and line up with the wave just before it begins to crest or break. If your paddling speed and location are in sync with the breaking wave, you can "catch" the wave. This is the moment when you don't have to paddle anymore, because the wave is doing all of the work (perhaps the most surreal feeling ever).

Once you catch a wave, you stand up, drop in, and begin to ride down the face, either to the right or the left of the breaking section.

Different surf spots have different types of waves. Some are beach breaks with sandy bottoms, much like the eastern coast of Florida, which creates consistent wave shapes up and down the coast. Others are reef breaks, like the Hawaiian Islands or many places in the South Pacific, where it gets shallow quite suddenly, causing immense, hollow, mammoth waves. Still other places, like Southern California, have rocky bottoms, providing a diversity of wave shapes and sizes. There are also point breaks, which only move in one direction, because the wave is breaking alongside a stretch of land that juts out into the ocean.

As you ride a wave, every move you make is in direct response to what the wave is doing. The best surfers in the world are the best, because they know how to respond to waves and transition quickly while riding.

Surfing is all about transition.

This is a lot like following Jesus. You never know which direction he's going to turn.

The Celtic Christians used to refer to the Holy Spirit as "the Wild Goose."

That's where the term "wild goose chase" came from. Walking with the Spirit was said to be like chasing a wild goose!

The Spirit is kind of like the sea, too. Always churning and teeming and moving with an energy that is beyond us. We don't create that energy. We don't control it. But if we're sensitive to its movement, we can have a pretty fun ride.

"The wind blows wherever it pleases. You hear its sound but you cannot tell where it comes from or where it is going. So it is with everyone born of the Spirit."

The Greek word for *Spirit* is *pneuma*, which means "wind" or "breath." It's similar to the Hebrew word *ruach*. It was the *ruach* that God breathed into Adam's nostrils in Genesis to give him life. It was to the *ruach* that Ezekiel was commanded to prophesy in order to turn a valley of corpses into a living army. The Spirit brings life. The Spirit animates. The Spirit is always moving, like breath being drawn in and released from our lungs.

FORWARD

As humans, the idea of movement can be difficult. We tend
to be more comfortable with predictability. Newton's first
law of motion states that an object in uniform motion tends
to stay in motion until an external force is applied to it. For
most of us, the force acting on us is not external but internal.
We're afraid, tired, skeptical, or maybe a bit lazy. Like a
snowball rolling toward the bottom of a hill, like that kid in
the movie *Hook*, who could fold his legs up to his chest and
roll like a bowling ball, or like a surfer nearing the beach at
the end of her ride, our motion tends to slow to a gentle stop
if the Spirit doesn't keep propelling us forward.

God is always moving things forward.

This is true of us as individuals and as communities. It's also
true of the people of God throughout history. God is moving
things along. Life is neither fixed nor static. God is the only
complete one. He's the absolute. Everything else in existence
bends and moves in response to him.

How many times have we tried to cling to the way things
used to be? The good old days. The golden age. If things
would just go back to the way they were back then. Let me
tell you something: Time moves forward. The narrative of
scripture is not leading us *back* to the Garden of Eden but
forward to a new garden-city. It's better. It's what that

original garden would have become if uninterrupted by brokenness and shame.

When we read the New Testament, we must embrace the challenge to contextualize it in the world in which we live. We can't go back to the first century. In reality, we wouldn't want to if we could. We have to believe that God is speaking and moving now, where we are, and he's pulling us forward into his glorious future.

Where is God going? Where is he leading us? Do we have hands that work miracles but ears that can't hear and eyes that can't see?

Maybe Jesus wants to reveal himself to you in a new way.

He might look like a ghost.

But give yourself a minute to recognize the voice of your savior out on the water, and embrace this new revelation as an invitation to join him on those shifting seas.

CHAPTER SIX

· · · · · · · · · ·

FIGHT

Kirby and I never fight.

That's a lie.

I've been told that all healthy couples know how to do conflict well. Maybe "fight" is too harsh of a word for you. Our premarital counselor, Pastor Bud, used to refer to marital fights as IFEs: "intense fellowship episodes."

I'd rather just call it what it is. A knock-down, drag out, Thunder Dome-style battle to the death. A fight.

Through the years, Kirby and I have learned how to fight better. We don't always get it right, but it's healthier than when we were younger.

When we first started dating, I remember starting to feel this strange, new emotion that I had not experienced much up to that point. I realize now it's called "anger."

I've never really been an angry person. I didn't struggle with anger before we started dating. But suddenly, I had this new feeling that swelled up in my chest when we started to argue. I didn't know what to do with myself!

One night, Kirby and I had a bad fight at my house. She got so frustrated that she jumped into her car and drove off.

Now, I've been told that you're not supposed to do that in a fight—walk away or drive off in your car. It's an unhealthy power move. I tried to tell her that. She didn't listen.

After she drove away, I was so angry that I tore a handful of leaves off a tree in the front yard and threw them as hard as I could. They only went a few feet in front of me and then drifted listlessly to the ground. Then I kicked the air like Chuck Norris.

Unsatisfying.

So I went into the backyard and started picking up bricks out of our fire pit and throwing them at an old oak tree. Surely that would make me feel better.

As I was rearing back to throw my second or third brick, I heard a burst of laughter from behind me. Kirby had only circled the block and come back to resolve our conflict. She heard me grunting from the backyard and walked in on my brick-throwing exercise.

We fight better now. We fight *for* each other. We fight *for* the relationship.

And it's been a while since I've thrown anything.

Most of us don't like to talk about conflict, because it makes us uncomfortable. We think conflict means there's something wrong with us.

We especially don't like the idea of having conflict with God. But when we look over the scriptures, we find a rich history of argument, debate, and fighting.

Sometimes people even throw things.

WRESTLING MATCH

In Genesis 18, God tells his friend, Abraham, that he is going to destroy Sodom and Gomorrah. What is Abraham's response?

"Well, you're God, so do what you're gonna do."

No! Abraham's nephew, Lot, lives in that city, so Abraham starts up a negotiation.

"Will you sweep away the righteous with the wicked? What if there are fifty righteous people in the city? Will you really sweep it away and not spare the place for the sake of the fifty righteous people in it? Far be it from you to do such a thing— to kill the righteous with the wicked, treating the righteous and the wicked alike. Far be it from you! Will not the Judge of all the earth do right?"

Abraham reminds God of his own character and holds him to it. "Far be it from you! Will Not the Judge of the earth do right?"

I love that. By the way, when we hear the word *Judge*, we might assume that means God is in the business of condemning people, but Isaiah defines God's judgment as "Settling disputes among peoples."

Eventually, Abraham gets the number down from fifty righteous people to ten. For ten righteous people, God will spare the entire city.

Now, we know how the story ends. The people of Sodom and Gomorrah try to sexually assault some angels, and the whole place goes up in smoke, leaving Lot's wife cemented in place as a pillar of salt and Lot's daughters tricking their father into getting them pregnant. (Just try and tell me the Bible is safe for the whole family. It's more like an episode of Jerry Springer.)

Later on, in Exodus 32, God tells Moses that he's angry at Israel, so he is going to leave them to finish their journey through the desert on their own. A little while earlier, the people had forced Moses's brother, Aaron, to build a golden calf that they could worship, because Moses was taking too long coming down from the mountain with the Ten Commandments. The scene looked something like Spring Break in Panama City Beach, Florida. Nothing but beads and body shots. It was a mess.

God is ticked, and rightly so, just like any parent would be if they were called down to the police station in the middle of the night to pick up their drunk teenage son.

So, when God tells Moses that he won't be completing the journey with them, how does Moses respond?

"Okay God. I respect your will."

No! He argues with him.

When God says, "Take the people you brought with you out of here," Moses, like our old friend, Abraham, holds God accountable by reminding him of his own character.

"These are *your* people . . . and we won't go without you."
Finally, God agrees to stick with them on the journey.

The list goes on. Jacob wrestles with God all night long on
the bank of a river, and in the morning, God gives him the
name, Israel, which means, "One who wrestles with God."

Mary convinces Jesus, the Son of God, to begin his ministry
before he's ready. They're at a wedding, and after everyone
is nice and sloppy, they run out of wine. Mary, knowing
that Jesus can make impossible things happen, tells him he
should fix the problem so the party can roll on.

His response: "My time has not yet come."

Like any loving mother, she ignores him and calls for the
waiters, telling them to do whatever Jesus tells them. I can
just imagine her pulling him up out of his chair and pushing
him toward the water basins.

We all know how that story ends. Water into wine. The party
turns into a rager, and the wedding planner looks like a hero.

REVERENCE

As followers of Jesus, we often shy away from this sort
of confrontation with God. I hear people talk a lot about
reverence and fear. Arguing with God would be irreverent,

right? That's the kind of thing that will get you a lightning bolt in the back or stuck in the belly of a fish.

But what if the argument is the point?

What if God wants us to confront him?

Have you ever noticed that, in those particular stories, Abraham and Moses look a lot like Jesus? Pleading the cause of the outsider, the underdog, the forsaken.

What if God delights in his children challenging him to act like himself? Reminding him that he is, in fact, slow to anger, abounding in love, rich in mercy, kind to the wicked and the ungrateful.

Jesus taught us to love our enemies. What happens when we ask God to do the same?

Are we afraid of the conversation? Maybe it's the very conversation he's been waiting for us to bring up.

INSTRUCTION

In 1 Corinthians 2, Paul quotes a famous passage from Isaiah 64. "'No eye has seen, No ear has heard, No human mind has conceived'—the things God has prepared for those who love him."

Then he follows that thought with his own rebuttal. "But God has revealed it to us by his Spirit."

Wow. So all the things that no eye has seen nor ear heard nor mind conceived, these are the things we can know by the Spirit of God. Interesting take, Paul.

He continues his thought by saying the Spirit searches the deep things of God and makes them known to us.

The final thought of the passage is the most amazing of all. Paul quotes Isaiah again: "Who has known the mind of the Lord that he may instruct him?"

Then, he answers Isaiah's ancient question by saying, "But we have the mind of Christ."

Incredible. Isaiah asked a question hundreds of years before that was meant to be a statement of awe and reverence. "Who has known the mind of the Lord that he may instruct him?" Then, hundreds of years later, this punk Paul answers his rhetorical question simply by saying, "Us."

We know the mind of the Lord that we may instruct him.

Now, before you get all bent out of shape about what I (and the Apostle Paul, by the way) just said, hear me (us) out.

The word *instruct* is an interesting one. The Greek word Paul uses here is *symbibazo*. Say it with me: Sim-bee-bah-zoe. One of the definitions of this word is "to unite or knit together in affection." The idea is not that you are telling someone what to do, because you have authority over them, like a professor in a college classroom or your supervisor at Starbucks. It's more like two close friends, or spouses even, reaching common ground out of love and respect for each other.

"Who has known the mind of the Lord that he may instruct him?"

We have. We can. This is our invitation in Christ.

This is what friendship with God looks like.

Abraham was considered God's friend. That same chapter in Exodus in which Moses argues with God says that God would talk to Moses "face to face, as one would speak to a friend."

The wrestling. The arguing. Throwing bricks at oak trees. It's all part of being in relationship.

Sadly, if we were to take a poll of our prayer life, I'm willing to bet we spend most of our interaction with God praying about things like money or work or that lady in the neighborhood who's a little too snooty for her own good.

We've been invited to know God's thoughts, and many of us are content with asking him to help us pay the bills. I don't want to be condescending toward anyone with legitimate financial needs. God has come through for Kirby and me in desperate situations more times than I can remember. God actually does care about that stuff. He wants us to bring our needs to him. But he also invites us into something much bigger.

To know his mind that we may instruct him. To look beyond our limited bubble. Our tiny sphere of influence. To enter into the conversation taking place at the heart of the universe.

THE DIVINE DANCE

At the center of the universe is a community. A relationship. Father, Son, and Holy Spirit. Three who are one. This mystery reaches beyond the limits of human language, but we do our best to understand it.

Most of us are familiar with the concept of the Trinity. Though the word *Trinity* does not appear in the Bible, the idea pops up all over the place. God revealed as three distinct persons.

For centuries, theologians and scholars have labored to come up with appropriate ways to talk about the mystery of the triune God. In the third century, Tertullian (What a name! Did they call him Tert for short? Or maybe Ulli?) was the first to use the word *Trinity*. He is quoted as saying, "God is one, but God is not alone." How great is that?

In the twelfth century, St. Bernard of Clairvaux spoke of the affection that exists between the Father and the Son. He said if the Father is the one who kisses, and the Son is the one who is kissed, then the Spirit is the kiss itself.

My favorite description of the Trinity comes from a Greek word that scholars started using in the eighth century: *Perichoresis*. The literal meaning of this word is "to rotate." Theologians use this word to describe the nature of the relationship of the members of the Trinity. The mutual affection, delight, and servanthood of the Father and the Son and the Spirit toward one another.

What's so amazing about this concept is that the circle of love and delight does not face inward but outward. The invitation to follow Jesus is actually an invitation to get swept up into the divine dance! To receive the love, affection, delight, and service of the God who is a community, and to enter into his life-giving flow. What an amazing invitation that is!

LAMENT

There's a strange dynamic in the Western church, where we

don't know how to be honest about the difficult things in life. Everyone smiles, shakes hands, and tells each other that everything in their life is "just great!" The reality is, we're really bad at being honest about the hard stuff. That is, about our real life.

We preached a sermon series at our church a few years ago, spearheaded by my friend, Matt Reynolds, that caused me to start thinking about the psalms (and what it means to have honest conversations with God) in a new way.

Over half the psalms are psalms of lament (as is the book of Lamentations, in case that isn't obvious). Think about that. Over half! They are the psalms that say things like, "You've forsaken me, God!" or "How long? Will you forget me forever?" or "Won't you slay my enemies?" and "Dash their children against the rocks!"

Dash their children against the rocks? That's a little intense, isn't it?

The Book of Psalms gives us a template for authenticity with God. Honest conversation.

Most of us believe, whether consciously or not, that brutal honesty will threaten our relationships, but the Psalms tell a different story. The Psalms tell us that honesty actually strengthens the relationship.

This is true in marriage, friendship, and especially in our relationship with God.

I'm a pretty positive, upbeat guy. I love to make people laugh. I like having a good time. For most of my twenties, as a pastor, I made it my full-time job to keep everyone around me positive and hopeful. If I were a character in the children's movie *Inside Out,* I was Joy. (Don't act like you haven't seen it.) I exerted an incredible amount of energy making sure everyone's spirits were high and their faith was strong.

I've heard it said that every preacher has just one message. That message comes through in various ways in different sermons, but for the most part, there's one big thing he or she is trying to say. For me, for years, that was a message of *faith.*

If we have enough faith, we can move mountains. Heal the sick. Raise the dead. With faith, we can change the world.

I preached it. I lived it. I saw a lot of amazing things happen. I saw miracles and healings. I saw mountains move.

But a few years ago, I started to see things a little differently. I have always loved 1 Corinthians 12—14, mainly because of all the talk of spiritual gifts and miracles. The fireworks. The sexy stuff. Healing. Prophecy. Boom! Pow! (Imagine those

last two words written in big yellow comic book letters.)
Over the past few years, as I have read and reread those old,
familiar passages, I feel like I have started to understand
them for the first time.

In chapter 13, Paul talks about "the most excellent way." The
way of love.

> If I speak in the tongues of men or of angels, but
> do not have love, I am only a resounding gong or
> a clanging cymbal. If I have the gift of prophecy
> and can fathom all mysteries and all knowledge,
> and if I have a faith that can move mountains,
> but do not have love, I am nothing. If I give all
> I possess to the poor and give over my body to
> hardship that I may boast, but do not have love, I
> gain nothing.

> Love is patient, love is kind. It does not envy,
> it does not boast, it is not proud. It does not
> dishonor others, it is not self-seeking, it is not
> easily angered, it keeps no record of wrongs. Love
> does not delight in evil but rejoices with the truth.
> It always protects, always trusts, always hopes,
> always perseveres.

> Love never fails. But where there are prophecies,
> they will cease; where there are tongues, they
> will be stilled; where there is knowledge, it will
> pass away. For we know in part and we prophesy
> in part, but when completeness comes, what is
> in part disappears. When I was a child, I talked

like a child, I thought like a child, I reasoned like a child. When I became a man, I put the ways of childhood behind me. For now we see only a reflection as in a mirror; then we shall see face to face. Now I know in part; then I shall know fully, even as I am fully known.

And now these three remain: faith, hope and love. But the greatest of these is love.

Wow. These three remain: faith, hope and love. But the greatest of these is . . . faith. Right? No?

Of course, I was familiar with this passage. It's been read in every wedding I have ever attended (or officiated)! I have loved this passage for years. But if you had looked at my life and listened to the way I talked and the sermons I preached, you might think that I believed faith was the most excellent way. Hope was a close second, because if today doesn't go the way you want, there's always tomorrow. And if that doesn't work out, there's always next week or next year. Hold on! Keep your head high and your hopes up! After faith and hope, love received a bronze metal, trailing somewhere in the distance.

Faith can move mountains. Faith can work miracles. Faith can change everything.

But love comes to us in the valley of despair. In the dark

night of the soul. Love comes and sits silently with us and refuses to walk away when things get tough.

I realize now that in an attempt to walk in great faith, I had failed to enter the honest conversation that love invites us into.

If I'm honest, much of my faith in God's ability to do the impossible was driven by a desire for convenience. It's so much easier if the mountain just moves than to have to journey through the wilderness around it.

NEW YEAR'S EVE

On New Year's Eve 2010, I received an unexpected phone call. Kirby's dad had suffered a massive heart attack and died in his sleep. He was fifty-two.

My wife is an incredible woman, and she really shines in moments of crisis. In that situation, she did what she normally does. She was strong for the people around her, and she took care of the details. She was there for her little sister, Nikki, who was seventeen at the time.

Side note: I don't know if you've ever lost a loved one, but the way we handle funerals in our culture seems a bit unfair. The people who were closest to the deceased are the ones who end up having to handle all the details of the funeral and viewing and everything. It all seems a bit overwhelming!

Because of everything she needed to attend to, it was months before Kirby really began to grieve the loss of her father. She grew up, like so many, a child of divorce and had never lived with her dad. That left her with an unfulfilled longing throughout her teen and young adult years. In an instant though, at age twenty-five, that longing was cemented into bitter regret. The relationship she had always wanted to have with her father was lost and gone forever.

On some nights, she would burst unexpectedly into weeping and groaning. She made sounds I had never heard before. What do you do in that moment? As her husband, I couldn't make her feel better. I couldn't fix it. Faith didn't offer much to the situation either. What was there to hope for? My only option was to sit with her and be present. To hold her silently in the dark as she cried.

Faith can move mountains, but love holds us in the dead of night.

28

In February of 2012, we decided it was finally time to have a baby. Kirby was born to be a mother. Children love her. She comes alive when she looks into a baby's eyes. She would have started having kids the day we got married if I had been on board. I, on the other hand, needed some time.

By 2012, we were in a good place to start trying. We were finally making enough money to try to keep another human being alive. It felt like the right time.

I had always just assumed that the moment we started trying, we would get pregnant. That's how it worked for all those teenagers on TV.

The first month went by. Nothing. Another month. Nothing. We assured ourselves that these things take time, and a fertility doctor wouldn't even see us until after a year of trying.

Over the next few months, I'm pretty sure we kept the pregnancy test industry afloat. I should have bought stock in e.p.t.

A year passed. Nothing.

I'm a man of faith, so I encouraged Kirby that we should keep trying, and pray more about it, too.

I know it takes more than prayer, but prayer can't hurt, right?

After two years of trying, we finally went to a fertility clinic and began undergoing testing and treatment. Fertility meds are hard on a woman's body. There are enough hormones and stuff moving around in there already, but add the extra ones, and it's a whole different ball game.

Throughout the first few months of our journey through infertility, I, like normal, tried to stay positive and upbeat, armed with Bible verses and positive statements and ready to pull them out whenever doubt or disappointment reared its ugly head. Every month, like clockwork, when we saw that little frowny face emoji on the pregnancy test (who decided that emojis were the best way to communicate for the first time whether or not you're going to have a baby?), I would recite my usual, "Next month, baby. Don't be discouraged." Like some sort of overly optimistic broken record.

It took a while for me to actually enter into the pain with Kirby. I can't imagine how alone she felt every time I combatted her sorrow with well-intentioned but ill-timed statements of hope.

In the summer of 2014, at the height of our fertility treatments, we discovered, that yet again, we were not pregnant. As I held Kirby in the kitchen, her tears soaking my T-shirt, I realized it had been twenty-eight months since we had started trying. She was twenty-eight years old at the time. There are also twenty-eight days in a month, which makes up a woman's, you know, cycle. It all felt very poetic and sad and yet somehow beautiful. I decided to write her a song as my way of entering into her pain and sorrow and disappointment. I took a break from trying to move all the mountains and just sat with my weeping wife in the valley of despair.

I called the song "28."

28 months and it seems we have nothing to show
They say that the best things in life
Are the things that come slow
You never wanted much
This one thing would be enough
28 heartbreaks and 28 miles to go

Don't be afraid
To dream again
Don't fight the tears in your eyes
Just let 'em fall
I'd rather have two of us here than nothing at all

28 days in the open sea, 28 nights
28 ships that could rescue us, all out of sight
No, we're not giving up
Not when it just takes one
28 years from now
All that is wrong could be right

Don't be afraid
To dream again
Don't fight the tears in your eyes
Just let 'em fall

I'd rather have two of us here than nothing at all

And I'm just gonna feel this with you
I'm just gonna hold you still
Tonight, I'm just gonna lay beside you here

Don't be afraid
To dream again
Don't fight the tears in your eyes
Just let 'em fall
I'd rather have two of us here than nothing at all
Don't waste your time casting blame
This is nobody's fault
I'd rather have two of us here than nothing at all

That song marked the beginning of me being real and honest and raw about my feelings throughout that journey. I realized it was okay to be sad about it. I realized it was okay to shake my fist at the heavens every now and then, to tell God how much it hurt, how bad it sucked.

My ability to be honest about the pain strengthened our marriage. It also created a new space for intimacy with God.

Most of us are afraid that our honesty will damage our relationships, but the Psalms are screaming at us, telling a different story, if only we'll listen. We learned as we studied the Psalms that honesty creates intimacy. That covenant creates the context for honest conversation. If I truly believe that God won't walk out on me when I get real about my feelings, I can be free to let it all out.

Psalms of lament are the voice of faithful men and women
of God who read the promises of Psalm 1, that the righteous
will prosper while the wicked perish, but have experienced a
different set of circumstances. Perhaps many of these psalms
exist to show us that the proverbs aren't always true. Job's
friends may not know what they're talking about. There
are more bends in the "straight and narrow path" than we
assumed.

My prayers began to change from obligatory thanks and
empty petitions to true laments and honest complaints.

"Where's my kid, God?"

"All of our friends are having their second or third. Why is
this so difficult for us?"

"We've given our lives to serve you. We're pastoring at a
church. We're sacrificing for your kingdom, and you can't
give us a baby?"

"We saved ourselves for marriage! I guarantee if we had done
it in college, we would have gotten pregnant! Why not now?"
I would love to tell you that, as I write this, my little boy or
girl is playing in the next room or taking a nap in Kirby's lap,
but it's 2016, and we still don't have a child. It's been over

four years, and here we are.

We're still disappointed. We still feel the pain. We're still sad. But we decided a long time ago to let the pain drive us toward God rather than away from him.

We arrived at the conclusion that God can handle our angry prayers, swear words, and ugly, snotty tears. (I'm talking about me here. Kirby, of course, is a beautiful crier.)

We've found that our honesty with God about this situation has allowed us to be thankful about all the other areas of life where we're bearing fruit in visible ways.

Rather than trying to move the mountain, to change the circumstances, I'm letting the circumstances change me.

I used to talk a lot about faith. Now I tend to talk more about love, because love makes room for honest conversations. Love lets you be where you are and doesn't judge you for it. Love sits with you in the valley and holds you through the dark night of the soul and then leads you by the hand around the unexpected bends in the road.

MAYBE THE FIGHT IS THE POINT

Through all of this, I've come to believe that maybe the fight is the point. Maybe the back-and-forth, face-to-face relational dynamic is where this whole "following Jesus" thing is leading us.

Maybe God is inviting us, like Jacob, to wrestle with him through the night.

Maybe Jacob's limp was a badge of honor.

Maybe an honest conversation is all God has ever wanted from us.

Are we simply telling him what we think he wants to hear? Hollow *hallelujahs* and empty *amens*?

Maybe sometimes the most appropriate place for a *hallelujah* is after we've thrown a few bricks.

· · · · · · · · · · ·

CHAPTER SEVEN

THEM

I grew up in the suburbs of Atlanta.

As a kid, life seemed normal. I didn't recognize there was anything wrong with my world until I was twelve or thirteen.

The summer after I finished sixth grade, my family and I moved to Southern California. It was like a dream come true for me. I had spent the past few years subscribing to surfing magazines. I would pore over the pages, tear out the fold-out poster from the center of each month's issue, and slap it up on my bedroom wall like papier-mâché. I had never been surfing before, but something inside me was drawn to it. That act of sliding down waves as they wound along the coast was mesmerizing.

I was also drawn to the image of life that was painted in

those magazines. Everything was so blue! The water in those photos was intoxicating. Professional surfers—guys like Kelly Slater, Andy Irons, and Rob Machado—were my heroes! Who cares about baseball cards? Give me *Surfing* magazine! I would memorize everything I could about all the best surf spots around the world. Pipeline. Cloudbreak. J-Bay.

Naturally, when my parents sat Sean and I down to ask us if we wanted to move to Southern California, we both shouted, "Let's go!"

"You'll have to leave all your friends behind," they warned us.

"We'll make new friends," I retorted. "Let's go!"

We made the move in June of 1997.

One year later, in the summer of 1998, we moved back to Georgia. When I say "moved back," I mean back to the same town, the same neighborhood, and the same house, just in time to start eighth grade. You should have seen the looks on my friends' faces when I got on the school bus that fall. It was like they were seeing a ghost!

Our year in California impacted me in ways I'm still figuring out. I got enough salt water in my veins that I think something changed in my chemical makeup. I learned how to surf and snowboard. I learned how to speak the language of the locals and make my life look a little like a page out of those magazines. And I learned that I could be friends with a lot of different types of people.

I had worked so hard to fit in with the surf culture of Southern California that I felt a little bit like an alien when I returned to Georgia. I had eradicated any semblance of a southern accent from my speech, and my hair was bleached from the sun.

I didn't really fit the mold of any particular social group in my school anymore, so for the next few years, I just hopped from one to the next. I couldn't help but notice how natural it was for people to segment themselves off into one group or another. I also couldn't help but notice how racially divided my school was.

For the most part, the white students stuck together, and the black students clustered in their own groups. Of course, there was a good deal of overlap, but the distinction was clear.

I can't tell you how many times, in my younger years, that I laughed nervously at a racial joke, not fully understanding the darkness that lurked behind it. I even told a few in some of my more shameful moments. I didn't realize that I was experiencing and even participating in a broken part of humanity that God was working to restore.

The book of Revelation contains a scene where people from every nation, every language, and every ethnicity are gathered around the throne worshipping the Lamb. This is an important image, because not only are all of these different people groups present, their differences are still visible. Their ethnicity and race and language are still intact.

Many people think that the answer to racism is that we all go "color blind" for the sake of harmony, no longer acknowledging our differences. But this way of thinking actually removes dignity rather than bestowing it. The beauty of this passage in Revelation is that diversity is celebrated, and in that place of celebration, unity is found.

It's only human to cling to people who are like us and distance ourselves from people who are different. It's natural to stick with what and who we know. When we look at the grand narrative of scripture though, we see a God who is moving across borders and languages and races to meet all kinds of people wherever they are and invite them to play a role in the symphony he is composing. In fact, that was the original calling of the Hebrew people.

BLESSING

When God called Abraham to himself, he promised that Abraham would be a father of many nations, that his offspring would outnumber the stars in the sky, and that, through Abraham's family, every family on Earth would be blessed.

This is a challenging promise, because the idea of "blessing every family on Earth" wouldn't have made much sense in Abraham's day. In the ancient world, being blessed was beneficial, because it gave your group, your family, your tribe, an advantage over others. You were more likely to win in battle, take the land, and live to fight another day.

So, when God promises to bless all other families through Abraham's family, he is promising to do something that Abraham probably would not have asked for on his own. Of course, the Israelites had a hard time following through with this calling, as generation after generation went by, and they continually insulated themselves from outsiders.

HOLY SHEET

This book started with a story about Peter and Cornelius and a sheet. This particular story is incredibly important for the conversation about God's heart for the "other," so I'd like to share a few more thoughts about it.

Let's start with a quaint, little beach town called Joppa. Luke tells us in the book of Acts that Peter was staying with a guy named Simon the tanner. (As opposed to Simon the paler. I'm sorry, I had to.) Simon lived in the city of Joppa. Joppa was a significant place for first-century Jews, as it has its own particular role in Jewish history.

You may remember from Sunday school, as well as all of your childhood nightmares, the story about Jonah being swallowed by a giant fish. God tells Jonah to go to Nineveh to preach to them. Jonah doesn't want to go to Nineveh, because, like every good Hebrew at the time, he hated the Ninevites. Nineveh was the capital of Assyria, the greatest enemy of Israel in Jonah's day.

Instead of obeying God, Jonah ran away to Joppa, hopped on a boat, got thrown overboard, got swallowed by a fish, got vomited up by said fish, and washed up on dry land. This series of events caused Jonah to do some serious soul searching (understandably), and he decided to go to Nineveh after all, as the Lord had commanded him (good idea).

For three days, Jonah walked around Nineveh preaching the same message. "Forty days from now, God will destroy you!" Heart-warming.

Surprisingly (to Jonah), the people of Nineveh repented, the Lord showed them mercy, and Jonah went outside the city and sulked like a sullen child next to a gourd. (You couldn't make this stuff up.)

Why am I telling you this story?

Because Peter was the new Jonah.

Jonah had an opportunity to be a part of God's plan to show mercy to the nations of the earth, the outsiders, the pagans, the heathens, the sinners, and he didn't want to be a part of it.

He ran.

Not because he was scared, but because he didn't want God to be merciful to the Ninevites. He even told God later on in the story that he knew he was "a gracious and compassionate God, slow to anger and abounding in love, a God who relents from sending calamity." And in the next breath, "Take away my life, for it is better for me to die than to live."

Can you believe that? This guy would rather die than live in a world where the wicked Ninevites could be shown mercy.

But Peter was the new Jonah. Standing on a rooftop in Joppa, looking at "something that looked like a sheet" (Thanks for the detailed description, Peter), he heard God say, "Don't call anything unclean that I have made clean."

The Peter/Jonah connection goes even further. Several times in the gospels, Jesus actually refers to Peter as Simon Bar-Jonah, which means "Son of Jonah." Other gospel references tell us Peter's father's name was John. What's going on here?

Did someone get their facts wrong?

All of the accounts where Peter is referred to as "Simon, son of Jonah" are actually different gospel references of the same account. Let's look at Matthew's perspective.

> When Jesus came to the region of Caesarea Philippi, he asked his disciples, "Who do people say the Son of Man is?"
>
> They replied, "Some say John the Baptist; others say Elijah; and still others, Jeremiah or one of the prophets."
>
> "But what about you?" he asked. "Who do you say I am?"
>
> Simon Peter answered, "You are the Messiah, the Son of the living God."
>
> Jesus replied, "Blessed are you, Simon son of Jonah, for this was not revealed to you by flesh and blood, but by my Father in heaven. And I tell you that you are Peter, and on this rock I will build my church, and the gates of Hades will not overcome it. I will give you the keys of the kingdom of heaven; whatever you bind on earth will be bound in heaven, and whatever you loose on earth will be loosed in heaven." Then he ordered his disciples not to tell anyone that he was the Messiah.

It's as if Jesus was saying, "Peter, I'm going to build my Church on your life. And it's not going to look the way you think. Much like Jonah, I'm going to send you to your worst enemies, the outsiders, the people your people can't stand, and you're going to have to decide how to respond, whether to view my mercy toward them with delight or with disdain."

Jonah's story is open-ended. It closes with God asking Jonah a question. "Nineveh has more than a hundred and twenty thousand people who cannot tell their right hand from their left, and many cattle as well. Should I not be concerned about that great city?"

How interesting is it that God describes the people of Nineveh, a city known for its violence and corruption, as those "Who cannot tell their right hand from their left"?

It reminds me of the prayer of Jesus on the cross. "Forgive them, father, for they know not what they do."

So, back to the rooftop. Peter heard the command of Jesus not to call anything unclean that God has called clean. This happened three times. Suddenly, three men showed up downstairs looking for Peter. Peter went with them, and they arrived in Caesarea three days after the angel told Cornelius to send for him.

Caesarea was a Roman outpost in Israel. It was filled

with statues of Caesar. It stunk of Rome. It represented everything the Jews of that day hated, a constant reminder of their oppressors. A present-day Nineveh.

After entering Cornelius's house, Peter began to talk about Jesus, and suddenly, the Holy Spirit moved in power throughout the house, and everyone present was filled with the Spirit.

Sound familiar? It was almost the same thing that had happened to the Jews who were gathered for the feast of Pentecost in Acts 2.

Acts 10:45 says, "The circumcised believers who had come with Peter were astonished that the gift of the Holy Spirit had been poured out even on the Gentiles."

Did you catch that? "*Even* on the Gentiles."

They couldn't believe it. Everything God had given the Jews who professed faith in Jesus was given to the outsiders. This had to be a difficult moment for Peter and the men who had come with him. They no longer had anything left to set themselves apart from the Gentiles. Nothing to make themselves feel superior. The playing field had officially been leveled.

A great conversion took place in Cornelius's home that

day. Cornelius, a God-fearing Gentile, was converted as he heard the good news of Jesus, as were the members of his household.

But they weren't the only ones who experienced a conversion.

Peter was converted, too. Peter experienced the real breadth and depth of the gospel for the first time that day, and his mind was changed. As he crossed the threshold into that Gentile house, he crossed into a whole new way of viewing the world.

"Can anyone keep these people from being baptized with water? They have received the Holy Spirit *just as we have*."

Baptism was a big deal. To baptize these Gentile believers was to make them members of the family of believers. Members of the Church. Gathered around the same table.

Word got out to the other apostles and church leaders around Judea, so they called a meeting with Peter. He told them everything that happened with the sheet and the animals and Cornelius and the Spirit.

"So then," the other apostles replied, "God has granted *even the Gentiles* repentance unto life."

In an instant, everything changed. Conversion. First for Cornelius. Then for Peter. Then for the other Christian leaders in Judea.

It's interesting to me that Peter and the other apostles thought they understood the full measure of God's love for humanity, then on a seemingly random afternoon, they were confronted with the reality that they hadn't even scratched the surface. They hadn't even begun their journey down the rabbit hole.

Conversion, by the way, simply means "to turn."

How many of us need a conversion today? How many times have I had to be converted since I started following Jesus? How many more conversions will I experience in my life?

How many times will God have to change my mind about something or someone or some group of people that I thought I had all figured out?

Following Jesus is about following a person, not a set of principles. This means he might appear to change course every once in a while. Are we willing to turn with him?

Who are your Ninevites?

Who is your Cornelius?

Who in this world is, by your estimation, so far from God that they are completely beyond reach?

Who in this world is so different, so disgusting, so foreign and unfamiliar that you wouldn't want them to spend ten seconds sitting at your dining room table?

What if those people were at Jesus's table?

Seriously, who are they?

What if God told you to go to those people to tell them how much he loves them?

What if God told you to have them over for Thanksgiving this year?

What if all those people who should know better are really those who don't know their right hand from their left? Those who know not what they do?

We need a conversion. A turning.

And conversion involves repentance. Changing our mind. The kingdom is at hand.

Close by.

Close to us.

Close to them.

WRATH

In Matthew 23, Jesus rebukes the Pharisees and teachers of the law, the insiders, the religious people, the ones who considered themselves to be in right relationship with God, for "shutting the kingdom of heaven in people's faces."

I don't want to be that person. Trying to keep someone out whom God is welcoming in.

He tells the Pharisees, "You are willing to cross land and sea to win a single convert just to make him twice as much a son of hell as you are."

In fact, most of Jesus' rebukes in the gospels are directed toward those who thought they were the insiders. Those who kept the *other* at a distance.

WHIPPING BOY

In an attempt to prove that Jesus can get angry and violent, I often hear people cite the account of Jesus flipping tables and driving everyone out of the temple with a whip. Great story.

Jewish salesmen had set up a market in the temple to sell animals for sacrifice. The people buying those animals had traveled a long distance to worship God and could not bring animals from home.

The salesmen, or moneychangers, were set up in a portion of the temple known as the Court of the Gentiles. Outsiders were allowed to worship at the temple, but they could only enter the outer court. The inner courts were reserved for true Jews.

Jesus saw his own people taking advantage of the outsiders, and he was furious. He flipped their tables. Coins flew everywhere. He fashioned a whip and drove everyone out of the court quoting Isaiah, "My house will be a house of prayer for all nations," and adding, "But you have made it a den of robbers."

Never in scripture is Jesus angrier than when the insiders take advantage of the outsiders, keeping them at a distance from the one who loves them.

Who are you keeping at a distance?

LIVING BRIDGES

A few years ago, while scouring the furthest reaches of the internet, looking for a decent sermon illustration, I stumbled across something astounding. In the depths of the jungle in the Indian state of Meghalaya are a series of *living bridges* that have been cultivated and grown by the local Khasi people for generations. The pliable root systems of the banyan fig trees have been redirected and woven together for years to form bridges that reach across canyons and rivers, connecting one village to another.

The process of growing a bridge (think about that idea for a second!) takes decades and is its own art form. One bridge might take thirty to fifty years to grow, but it could live for hundreds of years into the future. One woman might devote her entire life to the development of a single bridge, knowing that her children and grandchildren will cross that bridge daily, also devoting their lives to tending to its health and maturation.

What a beautiful picture of what can happen when we choose to *grow* bridges from one people group to another. From one person to another.

Bridges made of wood and steel and concrete will collapse, given enough time, but living bridges grow stronger with each passing year.

In the neighborhood where our church meets is a bridge that has been closed for years. We refer to it as "the bridge to nowhere." It just stops halfway across. It is a sad picture of the social chasm that exists between so many people groups.

The racial divide in the southern United States, especially in Atlanta, is disturbing. The effects of systemic sin from generations past remain to this day. So much has been done by great men and women who have gone before us. Dr. Martin Luther King, Jr. is a hero for the work he began in his short time in our city. A living bridge began to grow. Many others have come after him and dedicated their lives to the growth and maturity of that bridge.

But the work is not done yet. The canyon is wide, and the bridge is young. But when the ancient root systems from both sides direct their energy toward the other, the process is expedited, and if the appropriate amount of energy is applied for long enough, a thriving bridge can grow that will provide safe passage from one people to another for generations to come.

Most of us never knew that the roots of trees could create living architecture. We never realized that something we see all the time could meet a need that we face every day.

A concrete bridge can be erected in a few months, but a living bridge? That takes decades. Generations.

When I look at the lives of Dr. Martin Luther King, Jr., Nelson Mandela, Mahatma Gandhi, and Dietrich Bonhoeffer,

I start to think that it just might be worth it.

I'm reminded of the great *hall of faith* that is described in
Hebrews 11. The cloud of witnesses who cheer us on as we
run our race and grow our bridges. Those who left everything
they had, who gave everything.

Each was seeking the city to come, not a city of man but the
city of God, where every tribe and tongue will be gathered as
one.

The author of Hebrews says that God is not ashamed to be
called their God, that the world was not worthy of them, and
that only together with us can their work be made complete.

Where are the canyons in your world? Where do chasms
exist between peoples?

What would it be like to give your life for the development of
a bridge? Not a bridge made of concrete and steel but a living
bridge.

A bridge made of flesh and blood and tears and laughter and
breath and love.

CHAPTER EIGHT

....

HERE

My dad is an Eagle Scout. I say *is* rather than *was,* because once an Eagle Scout, always an Eagle Scout.

When I was a kid, my parents signed me up for Cub Scouts. You know, where little boys build bonfires and learn to tie knots. Life skills. You start in first grade with Tiger Scouts, then Bobcats, then Wolf Scouts, and then Bear Scouts. I made it all the way to Webelo. (By the way, what kind of a word is "Webelo"? Sounds like some weird animal from a Dr. Seuss book.) Then I quit, because I was tired of wearing khaki shirts, and I expected way more knife activities at our weekly meetings.

Growing up in the house of an Eagle Scout meant we did a lot of outdoor activities. My dad still holds tightly to a few scouting values, which he engrained into my childhood. The first is "Always be prepared." No kidding. My dad is always the guy with the enormous cooler full of drinks and food. He always remembers where he parked his car in a confusing parking garage. And, even with an iPhone in his pocket, he keeps a giant Rand McNally book of maps of every city in America under the passenger seat of his truck.

The second value is "Leave it better than you found it." This means that whenever we went camping, we would clean up any excess trash when we were packing up, even if it was there when we arrived. It's a simple rule, and I've found my dad applies it to other areas of life as well.

In our neighborhood growing up, my dad was the one who mowed not only his own lawn but also the common spaces around the neighborhood pool and tennis court. He went over and above. He took initiative and ownership. He still does today.

SOMEWHERE ELSE

For many Christians, when they talk about heaven, the afterlife, where we will go when we die, they tend to talk about *going away* to *somewhere else*. There's a disconnect between the world we inhabit now and the one we will occupy for eternity. We speak of pearly gates and clouds and harps. We picture fat, little angel babies with halos and white nightgowns.

While some of this imagery appears in the Bible (kind of),
scripture paints a very different picture of the age to come.

To understand where this thing is going, we need to
understand where it started. At the beginning of Genesis,
God places Adam and Eve in a garden and gives them the
charge to *cultivate*. That word, *cultivate*, is interesting. It's
an agricultural term. One of the definitions of the word is "To
foster growth." It's where we get the word *culture*. The idea
was that Adam and Eve were not only to grow crops but also
to build culture.

In partnership with God, they were to create a world where
life would flourish, where culture would develop, and where
humanity would mature toward its destiny.

When we look at the end of the Bible, we see a similar,
yet different, image: a city coming down from heaven and
resting firmly on our planet. The new Jerusalem. A garden
city.

Much like the garden from the first story, the river of
the water of life is there. On its banks sits the tree of life.
Only this time, there are not one but two trees of life, each
yielding fruit in and out of season and whose leaves are for
the healing of the nations. Within that city are people from
every tribe and tongue. There is no more sickness, no more
violence, no more greed. Only light and love and the glory of

God's face.

The second garden, the garden city, is certainly a work of God. A miracle. But it seems this is what the original garden would have become had Adam and Eve resisted temptation and continued in their vocation to cultivate and subdue.

What we see in these passages, and many others, is that heaven does not exist in some other place, in a land far, far away. It exists right here on Earth.

SWORDS AND SHOVELS

A child can turn just about anything into a weapon. Earlier, I mentioned my obsession with ninjas. Growing up, I had swords stashed all over my house. Some of them were fresh from the toy aisle, while others were of the makeshift variety. To a little boy, basically, anything long and pointy can be a sword. A stick. A wooden spoon. A TV remote.

And don't get me started on guns. We had nerf guns, water guns (Who remembers the Super Soaker 2000? It had a shoulder strap and everything!), paintball guns, and BB guns.

One time, I was walking through the woods with my friend, Josh, and he was carrying a BB gun.

"Hey, let me shoot you in the back of the leg," he said. "It won't hurt, 'cause I'll only pump it once."

"Okay."

He pumped the gun one time and shot me in the leg. It felt like I had been stabbed by a flaming blow dart! (He had already pumped the gun ten times before asking me.)

Violence, to some degree, is part of the human experience. It's in our culture. It's in our media. It's in our bones. But the prophet Isaiah promises a day when all of our swords will be bent into plowshares. When all the clothing and equipment used for war will be fuel for the fire. It's as if he's saying that every instrument of violence and destruction will be repurposed so it can be used for human flourishing.

This promise goes a lot further than toy swords and BB guns. What about AK-47s? Drones? The A-bomb? Imagine what it would look like if we invested the technology, the intelligence, and the finances that go into developing and producing things that kill into things that heal. Things that build. Things that restore.

Isaiah also promises a day when the nations will stream to Mount Zion so they may learn to walk in the ways of the Lord. Can you imagine that? A day when the leaders of every nation will get together and say, "You know what? Those

Jesus people seem to have something figured out. Let's go learn from them."

All of this certainly amounts to more than simply telling people how to go to a certain place when they die. It's about learning how to live.

PEOPLE FROM THE FUTURE

If heaven is a future reality that will exist one day on this planet, marked by peace, love, joy, and forgiveness, what happens if we start to live that way right now?

This is what most of Jesus's teachings are about. Loving our neighbor. Forgiving those who sin against us. Praying for our enemies. The narrow gate. The way. The truth. The life.

Dallas Willard describes eternal life as "the eternal kind of life." Isn't that interesting? This sort of life has a quality that we are invited to start living today.

What if we can live the life of heaven now?

In the midst of a world marked by violence, selfishness, greed, and ambition, we can live a life of love and selflessness.

In doing so, we live as people from the future. A sign and a wonder. A revelation of what is to come.

One day, the earth will be filled with the knowledge of the glory of God, but until that day, we have the opportunity to reveal it. One day, the nations will come to God's city to learn how to live. A city whose gates are always open and whose lights are always on will possess trees that will bear fruit year round and whose leaves can heal the nations. But today, we can bear the fruit of the Spirit.

We can grow love, joy, peace, patience, kindness, goodness, faithfulness, gentleness, and self-control. These are the natural products of a life planted in God. A branch that abides in the vine.

So many Christians are just holding on until the end. Waiting to get rescued. To meet Jesus in the sky so he can right all the wrongs in the world.

What if he is waiting for us to do it? To begin cultivating again. To start bending swords into shovels. To start taking our leaves out of the city gates and offering them to the nations of the world.

What if our leaves can heal? What if our fruit can reveal a better way?

I think that's why Peter describes his fellow first-century

believers as "aliens and strangers here." We're supposed
to be different. We're time travelers. Living the way of the
future. Living the life of heaven.

Imagine, for a moment, that you found yourself in a *Back to
the Future* scenario, where a crazy old man with a souped-
up DeLorean sent you fifty years into the past. What about a
hundred years? A thousand years? Imagine the tension you
would feel living in a time when people didn't have high-
speed internet, when schools were still segregated, when it
was normal for some people to own other people. You would
lose your mind!

Sadly, we don't have to travel back in time to feel that
tension. All of those things are a present reality somewhere
on Earth right now. Even in "the land of the free," there are
people who are currently not afforded some basic civil rights.
Some have referred to this tension as the *now but not yet*
of the kingdom of God. We have heard the promises of the
beautiful future, but we live in the broken reality of the now.
Within us though, we carry proof of what's to come.

This must be why Jesus said, "The kingdom of God is *within*
you."

G. K. Chesterton wrote poetically about the cross and the
resurrection of Jesus as a moment of transition in human
history.

On the third day the friends of Christ coming
at daybreak to the place found the grave empty
and the stone rolled away. In varying ways they
realized the new wonder; but even they hardly
realized that the world had died in the night.
What they were looking at was the first day of a
new creation, with a new heaven and a new earth;
and in a semblance of the gardener God walked
again in the garden, in the cool not of the evening
but the dawn.

What if we began to view the cross and the resurrection from
this point of view? The old world died, and a new world is
breaking forth. If you're like me, you might be thinking,
"Yeah, that's really inspiring, but when I look around, I still
see the old world."

When we look outward, we are overwhelmed with reports of
violence and oppression, injustice and greed. The old world
appears to be alive and well.

When we turn inward, we see our own darkness. Ambition,
deceit, anger, and lust. The old self lurks in the shadows.

But just as the light appears before the sun breaches the
horizon at daybreak, we can also see the evidence of a new
creation emerging. The future spilling into the now.

Like a seed that has been buried but is not yet a great tree, we can see a tender green shoot piercing the soil. Or, like Elijah, we may view through squinting eyes a cloud the size of a man's hand in the distance, and still possess the confidence that the rains of heaven are only moments away.

Maybe this is what it means to be people of faith. To carry the substance of things hoped for. To know that a world exists within us that will one day exist around us. To believe that a tiny mustard seed is enough to provide shade for an entire garden. To be confident that a single act of forgiveness, patience, or kindness can carry within it the weight of an entire kingdom.

What if we began to see ourselves as people from the future, leaders, pioneers, sent ones who are living in the present with a purpose?

People sent to cultivate this world once again, leaving it a little better than we found it.

· · · · · · · · · ·

WHISPERS IN
DARKENED HALLWAYS

We've talked about Beanie Babies and treehouses and night terrors and true selves and surfing and lamenting and living bridges and Webelos. We've established the idea that God is still speaking. He's always speaking. Not just to individuals but to entire communities, entire generations.

The question has never been, "Does God have something to say?" but "What is he saying?"

My intentions with this book are not tell you what I think God is saying, to tell you what these Wind Words are, but to invite you to listen.

What is God saying?

What are the Wind Words?

In your neighborhood.

In your community.

In your country.

In your home.

What conversations are you having?

So many of these conversations started out for my friends and I as whispers in darkened hallways and stairwells and living rooms.

What is God really like? What is he saying? Could he really be as good as we hope? Could he really be different than we thought and better than we feared?

One person would stumble upon a passage of scripture or read a book or have a conversation that got them thinking, and then they would tell another person. Before long, our entire community was whispering in darkened hallways, one person to another, one conversation at a time.

A NEW RENAISSANCE

Most of us are familiar with the Renaissance period that brought European culture out of the Middle Ages and into modernity. Beginning sometime in the fourteenth century in Florence, Italy, following the Black Plague, and ending in the seventeenth century, the Renaissance touched every sector of society. Art, literature, music, science, philosophy, politics, religion—a revolution took place in each area.

The word *Renaissance* means "rebirth" in French, and while there is much debate over whether or not all of the effects of this process were positive, everyone agrees that the world has never been the same since.

Is it possible that we're on the verge of a new renaissance? Another rebirthing of culture, science, and religion?

Certainly technology has brought about massive changes to our world over the past fifty years. Globalization has connected us in ways we could never have imagined. Of course, it has its negative effects, too. In a world where I can be Facebook friends with a pastor in Africa or a musician in Denmark, I can also fail to learn the names of my next door neighbors.

The Protestant Reformation in the fifteenth and sixteenth centuries changed church life and theology around the world, as men like Martin Luther, John Calvin, and Huldrych Zwingli challenged the religious status quo.

Are we on the cusp of a new reformation?

As I talk to men and women from around the world, I hear similar conversations emerging.

What if the conversations we are having could impact the way people think about God for hundreds of years?

What if our discovery of what God is like could bring liberty and peace and reconciliation and empowerment for the world in which our children and grandchildren and great-grandchildren grow up?

I want to be part of *those* conversations.

One social structure that arose during the Renaissance was the *salon*. No, not the place where middle-aged woman get their hair done and share juicy gossip with each other. Deriving its name from the French word for "living room" or "parlor," a salon was a gathering in someone's home for the purpose of enjoying art and poetry and for the exchanging of new and intriguing ideas.

Salons were popular among the social elite at the time. Though they possessed an air of exclusivity, the image of this sort of gathering is powerful. A group of friends and neighbors assembling in a home to celebrate the creative work of local artists and writers and *whispering about what could be.*

Politics, philosophy, religion. The static structures at the time were questioned, and dreams of a better way were shared among friends.

What would it look like to make the salons of sixteenth-century France and Italy a part of your community in Chicago, San Francisco, Omaha, Sydney, Stockholm, Quito, Cape Town, or Seoul? What would it look like to gather your friends and family and neighbors and ask, "What are the Wind Words?" "What is God saying?"

I told you at the beginning of this journey together that this was not going to be a book full of answers. I'm not here to tell you what the Wind Words are. I just want to remind you that Jesus is speaking. He's writing a letter to his churches. He might be writing a letter to your church. Your community. Your house. Your salon.

He's inviting you into the conversation.

So we'll end this book the way we started it, with one simple question.

Are your ears awake?

REFERENCES AND RAMBLINGS

· · · · · · · · · ·

INTRODUCTION

The Apostle Paul's sentiments: This comes from his famous poem about love from 1 Corinthians 13.

Rooftops and Reptiles: The story about Peter seeing the vision of the sheet and then visiting Cornelius' house comes from Acts 10.

Jesus' command to "go to the ends of the Earth": This comes from Matthew 28 and is widely known as "the Great Commission."

"Are your ears awake? Listen. Listen to the Wind Words, the Spirit blowing through the Churches." This question and statement appear seven times throughout Revelation 2 and 3 in *The Message*.

You can follow Pope Francis on Twitter at @pontifex. Read that sentence again. What a time to be alive!

1: WORD

Drew and Caroline McClure lead a discipleship program for college students in Colorado called Sojourn. They also started the Summer Discipleship Project in Myrtle Beach, South Carolina, as a part of the college ministry at our home church, Grace Midtown.

Religious practice isn't a bad thing. It was the strength of tradition that allowed the Roman Catholic Church to survive the Dark Ages. I've found great encouragement through difficult seasons of life by practicing spiritual disciplines. It's when it becomes a lifeless obligation or a checking of boxes that we start to have problems.

The Brennan Manning quote is from his book *The Ragamuffin Gospel*. Read it. It will rock your face off.

Confession: I actually enjoy reading *GQ* and looking at Pinterest and watching Ryan Gosling movies. I had too much pride to say it earlier, but I'm coming clean here, because I'm betting fewer people will read this part of the book.

Beanie Babies: I'm pretty sure I still have a Bubbles the Fish somewhere that is worth something like $1,000.

The Jesus-y Kanye West song is called "Jesus Walks," and it appeared on his 2004 debut album *The College Dropout*. "Gold Digger" appeared on his 2005 follow-up album, *Late Registration*, and featured Jamie Foxx on vocals.

The honey mustard in my Bible is most likely from Chick-fil-a.

The clothing and shoes of the Israelites: This story appears in Deuteronomy 8:4 and 29:5.

"In the beginning was the Word." This passage appears in John 1.

One of my favorite quotes about Jesus being the Word of God comes from Brian Zahnd: "Jesus is what God has to say." How great is that?

Moses the humblest: This appears in Numbers 12:3.

"Jesus is the image of the invisible God" appears in Colossians 1.

"The radiance of God's glory and the exact representation of his being" appears in Hebrews 1.

"The law was given through Moses, but grace and truth came through Jesus" appears in John 1.

"At one time God spoke through angels and prophets, but now he has spoken *by* his Son" appears in Hebrews 1.

I first heard the phrase "Words, works, and ways" from Mike Breen. Check out his books *Building a Discipling Culture* and *Family on Mission*, to name a few.

LeVar Burton was the host of a popular educational television program in the early 1990s called *The Reading Rainbow*. He used to end every episode by saying, "But don't take my word for it." I think he was also the pilot on *Star Trek*.

To read the Bible is to interpret the Bible: I first encountered this concept in Gordon Fee and Douglas Stuart's book *How to Read the Bible for All Its Worth*.

Warby Parker is a great company and makes some pretty cool glasses. Check them out at warbyparker.com.

"Jesus may live in your heart, but grandpa lives in your bones" is actually a quote from Pete Scazzero. He is known for writing the *Emotionally Healthy* series. You can learn more at emotionallyhealthy.org.

"The God who is love": 1 John 4:8 and 4:16 tell us "God is love."

Rorschach Test: I first heard Jonathan Martin describe the book of Revelation as a Rorschach test that reveals more about the reader than about the text itself. I thought it was an amazing concept, so I took the liberty of applying it to all of scripture. Thanks, Jonathan!

Interpreting the Bible through the lens of Jesus: This way of viewing the scriptures has been referred to as "The Jesus Hermeneutic."

"God is much different than we thought and much better than we feared" comes from Richard Rohr's book *Things Hidden*. Be careful before you read it. It will ruin your life.

Greek words: *sarx*, *logos*, and *ginosko*. BlueletterBible.org is an excellent online resource for Greek and Hebrew word studies.

2: FATHER

Ninjas: Some of the movies that came out during that time period include *Teenage Mutant Ninja Turtles*, *Teenage Mutant Ninja Turtles II: The Secret of the Ooze*, *Teenage Mutant Ninja Turtles III*, *Three Ninjas*, *Three Ninjas Kick Back*, and my personal favorite (for obvious reasons), *Surf*

Ninjas.

The burning bush appears in Exodus 3.

The term "progressive revelation" is often used to describe the way God's deep nature unfolds over time throughout the narrative of scripture. Abraham didn't get the whole picture. Moses only got the next chapter. Only in Jesus is God made fully known.

"Our Father," often referred to as "The Lord's Prayer": These words are found in Matthew 6:12 and Luke 11:4.

"Show us the Father" appears in John 14.

"If you, then, though you are evil, know how to give good gifts to your children . . ." appears in Matthew 7:11 and Luke 11:13.

"Take this cup from me" appears in Matthew 26:49 and Luke 22:42.

A better name: I was at a Jason Upton concert when God spoke to me about having a better name for him. Jason probably did more talking than singing that weekend, and I might have heard God's voice more in those few hours than I had all year! Check out his music at jasonupton.net.

Downton Abbey is a BBC original series that has taken the world by storm. Never in my life did I think I would care so much about the incompetence of the new footman or whether a wealthy heiress would ever find love again.

"Living in awareness of our belovedness": This Brennan Manning quote is from his book *Abba's Child*.

Tim Keller talks about the parable of the prodigal God in his book *Prodigal God*.

doulos: The concept of a bondservant comes from Exodus 21:5.

A few years ago, my friends Pat and Tony wrote a song called "Good Good Father." If you haven't heard it, you might be living in a hole or in a 1976 VW minibus with no radio or something. There's a reason this song has touched so many people. God is a father.

3: CLOSE

The *Left Behind* series, a string of post-apocalyptic Christian fiction books and movies, came out when I was in high school and set the tone for the way many Evangelicals approached eschatology for the next ten to fifteen years. A reboot starring Nick Cage was released last year, which makes perfect sense.

Matt Damon starred in *The Martian*, the 2014 film about an astronaut who leads the first NASA mission in years to find a habitable planet for the human race. Wait, that was *Interstellar*. What was *The Martian* about?

The college and young adult ministry we led was called theDoor (typed without a space between the words, because . . . I'm actually not sure why).

"Look up at the heavens and the stars" comes from Genesis 15:5.

The Leo DiCaprio movie is *Inception*, if there was any chance you didn't know that already.

Into the Silent Land: Anyone who is looking for an entrance into contemplative prayer should start here.

Dietrich Bonhoeffer, a German pastor who was executed in a Nazi concentration camp just weeks before WWII came to an end, wrote such classics as *Life in Community* and *The Cost of Discipleship*.

Cancelled the written code: This passage appears in Colossians 2:14–15.

The Beloved Disciple: This is John's self-given nickname. Talk about being in touch with your identity!

"Trade up your understanding" is a phrase I've only ever heard used by Tyler Thigpen.

"Accept that you are accepted" is a quote from Paul Tillich, used by Brennan Manning, and referred to often by my friends and I.

4: IMAGE

Chuck Norris is an American actor and martial artist who is well known as the star of *Walker Texas Ranger*, as well as for his signature Total Gym, and then more recently for a series of jokes that all revolve around how amazing, intimidating, and powerful he is. E.g., "Chuck Norris doesn't sleep. He waits." He also has a ginger mullet.

The creation poem can be found in Genesis 1 and 2.

Dallas Willard's use of the phrase "Creation Covenant" comes from his book, *The Divine Conspiracy*. Read everything he has ever written.

The false self: For more resources on this topic, check out Thomas Merton's *New Seeds of Contemplation*, Richard Rohr's *The Enneagram: A Christian Perspective*, and Pete Scazzero's *Emotionally Healthy Spirituality*, to name a few.

The Jonathan Martin quote about personas and persons

originally appeared in a tweet in 2014.

Snow-covered dung: My buddy, Drew, mentioned above, compares this to telling his wife, "Honey, you're disgusting, and I can't stand to look at you, but I found a solution. Whenever I see you, I just picture your sister, and I can tolerate you." Yikes! You can watch one of his sermons on this topic at https://vimeo.com/148106155.

Jacob and Esau: You can read about these twins starting in Genesis 25.

Cleaning the outside of the dish: Read about this rebuke in Matthew 23.

Immanuel: This prophecy is found in Isaiah 7 and 8.

Can I borrow your hand sanitizer? The passage about hand washing can be found in Mark 7.

To those who overcome: This passage is found in Revelation 3.

The eternal kind of life: I first saw this phrase in Dallas Willard's *The Divine Conspiracy*.

My wife's voice: Check her out at housefires.org and kirbykaple.com. Seriously, she's amazing.

Jesus the carpenter: There's a lot of speculation as to what it actually meant for Jesus to be a carpenter. He could have been a stonemason. Some have argued that the best interpretation of the word used to describe his vocation is something like a "day laborer."

Jesus had a job: My buddy, Pat Barrett, has preached some great messages about the incarnation and what it teaches us about being present in our own life. Check out his message, "Be Here," at https://vimeo.com/148881064.

The C. S. Lewis quote comes from his book, *The Weight of Glory.*

5: MOVEMENT

Ezekiel's vision of the river is found in Ezekiel 47.

Mrs. Gren: Mike Breen puts this acronym to great use in his book *Building a Discipling Culture.*

Snakes on a Plain: My buddy, Matt Reynolds, preached an insightful sermon about the bronze snake called "Listening Forward." You can watch it at https://vimeo.com/135895947. There's also a movie starring Samuel L. Jackson called *Snakes on a Plane* that I don't suggest watching.

The rich, young ruler is found in Matthew 19 and Mark 10.

My mother and brothers: This passage can be found in Matthew 12, Mark 3, and Luke 8.

"He intended to pass by them": This story is found in Mark 6.

"I never knew you": This statement is found in Matthew 7.

Chasing the goose: Mark Batterson wrote the book, *Wild Goose Chase,* about this idea.

"The wind blows where it pleases": Jesus spoke these words to Nicodemas in John 3.

Ezekiel's valley of dry bones can be found in Ezekiel 37.

The garden city can be found in Revelation 21.

6: FIGHT

Throwing bricks: I don't suggest throwing stuff when you're angry.

"Settling disputes among peoples" appears in Isaiah 2.

Jacob's wrestling match is in Genesis 32.

Jesus gets bossed around by his mom in John 2.

"At the center of the universe": I first read this phrase in
Darrell Johnson's *Experiencing the Trinity*.

Lament: The psalms quoted here are Psalm 22, 13, 143, and
139. My friend, Matt Reynolds, has a great message about
the psalms and honest conversations with God that you can
watch at https://vimeo.com/141372693.

The most appropriate place for a *hallelujah*: I first heard
John Goldengay present this idea based on his observation
that many (though not all) psalms of lament end as psalms of
thanksgiving.

7: THEM

Holy Sheet: This story comes from Acts 10.

Peter is the new Jonah: I first heard Buddy Hoffman connect
Peter and Jonah years ago in a sermon at Grace Fellowship
Church.

Simon, Son of Jonah: This passage is found in Matthew 16.

"They know not what they do": The prayer of Jesus from the
cross is found in Luke 23.

A great conversion: Justo Gonzalez gives a great explanation of this event in his book, *Santa Biblia: The Bible Through Hispanic Eyes.*

Whipping boy: This account appears in Matthew 21, Mark 11, and John 2.

"A house of prayer for all nations": This statement is from Isaiah 56.

Living Bridges: The BBC published an article about this a few years ago. You can read it at http://www.bbc.com/travel/ story/20150218-indias-amazing-living-root-bridges. Or just Google "living bridges Meghalaya." You won't believe your eyes.

8: HERE

Somewhere Else: Read N. T. Wright's *Surprised by Hope.* It will blow your mind hole.

"Cultivate": Tim Keller describes our human vocation in his book *Center Church.*

The first garden is found in Genesis 1 and 2.

The garden city is found in Revelation 21 and 22.

Swords and Shovels: The passage about bending swords into plowshares and nations streaming to Mount Zion appears in Isaiah 2.

The teachings of Jesus: Matthew 5—7, often referred to as "The Sermon on the Mount," describes the way of love and forgiveness.

"The eternal kind of life": Once again, I suggest reading *The Divine Conspiracy* by Dallas Willard.

Filled with the knowledge of the glory of God: This passage appears in Habakkuk 2.

Paul's list of the fruit of the Spirit appears in Galatians 5.

Abide in the vine: This language appears in John 15.

"Aliens and strangers" appears in 1 Peter 2.

"The kingdom of God is within you" appears in Luke 17.

The G. K. Chesterton quote comes from his book, *The Everlasting Man*.

"A cloud the size of a man's hand" appears in 1 Kings 18.

"Substance of things hoped for" appears in Hebrews 11.

ACKNOWLEDGEMENTS

. . . .

Kirby – You've been my ceaseless support and constant companion throughout this process, and long before it ever began. You're the one who's said for years that I need to write some stuff down. Thanks for holding me to it. Also, thank you for letting me use you for so many illustrations. It got a little ridiculous. For ever and ever, babe.

Mom, Dad, and Sean – I wouldn't trade my childhood or my family for anything in the world. These pages are filled with stories and adventures that have made me who I am. Sean, thanks for being cool about me telling the sleep walking story.

Matt, Pat, Drew and Chris – Five Aces! This book wouldn't exist if it weren't for you guys, and the ideas that I have been exposed to and confronted with through our *whispers in darkened hallways* and late night porch hangs. Your love for God, open hearts, faithful study and courage to pioneer are responsible for so much of this content. Who knows how many of these ideas are even my own? Thanks for letting me borrow (steal) from you!

Margaret and Justin – Your prophetic insight into the heart of God and the human soul have shaped my thinking so much over the past few years. Keep being deep wells.

Grant and Krissy – Your friendship and support through the years has meant the world to me, and so much of my personal story that appears in these pages was colored by your presence in my life. Forever friends.

My Grace Midtown family – Thank you for your openness and your courage to follow Jesus out on the water, even when he looks like a ghost. So many of these ideas were able to be developed in your midst because you have provided a safe place to listen to the Wind Words and seek to articulate what we're hearing. This story is *our* story, and it's not over yet!

Kevin – Thanks for your editing prowess and helping me not sound dumb. Hope it worked!

I'd also like to thank coffee, Apple products, the World Wide Web and noise cancelling headphones. I couldn't have done it without you.